'Reflecting deeply on recent historical approaches to management and organization studies, the authors have provided a uniquely reflexive account of the different histories, conceptions of histories and authors involved in recent scholarship that has sought to bring history back into focus in a largely ahistorical and instrumental field. The book will be a significant guide for those researchers seeking to disentangle the different approaches to histories involved in recent research, alerting them to the grounds and assumptions underlying various contributions.'
—*Stewart Clegg, Distinguished Professor of Management and Organization Studies at the University of Technology Sydney, Australia*

'There are no scholars better placed to explore the development of management and organization history studies than Albert Mills and Milorad Novicevic. They have made enormous contributions to the debates that have nourished this fascinating field of study over the years. In this book they chart an exciting and ambitious course for its future.'
—*Todd Bridgman and Stephen Cummings, authors of* A New History of Management

'This well-written and thought-provoking publication addresses its central topics as no book before and is a must read for those interested on management and organizations.'
—*Rafael Alcadipani, EAESP-FGV, Brazil*

'History needs to be taken seriously in management and organization research, and Mills and Novicevic do just that. The books offers a thought-provoking critical analysis of the reasons and consequences of the ahistorical orientation in management and organization research. By so doing, this book adds to the recent historical turn and helps us to go deeper and further than what we typically think organization or management history is all about.'
—*Eero Vaara, Professor of Organization and Management at Aalto University, Finland*

'This book provides deep insights on positivist and postmodernist historiography and demonstrates the role of historians in the authorship of history production in management and organization.'
—*⌐⌐an Deep Sharma, University School of Management Studies, India*

T0371796

Management and Organizational History

Management and organizational history has grown into an established field of research with competing and contrasting approaches and methods that are relevant for management and organization studies.

This short-form book provides readers with expert insights on intellectual interventions in management and organization history. The authors illuminate the central ideas, works, and theorists involved in forming the link between history, management, and organization studies, particularly focusing on the debates addressing the need for a 'historic turn' in management and organizational studies.

With coverage of nascent schools of thought in management historiography, such as ANTi-History, revisionist history, counter-history, Rhetorical History, the Copenhagen School, microhistory, critical realist histories, alongside existing modernist and post-modernist approaches, as well as postcolonial, decolonial, and feminist critiques, the book is essential reading for scholars and students learning or exploring the role of history in management and organization studies.

Albert J. Mills is a Professor of Management at Saint Mary's University (Canada) and Professor of Innovation Management at the University of Eastern Finland. He is also the co-editor of the journal *Qualitative Research in Organizations and Management*.

Milorad M. Novicevic (PhD, University of Oklahoma) is a former Chair of the Academy of Management – History Division and an Associate Professor at the University of Mississippi.

State of the Art in Business Research
Edited by Professor Geoffrey Wood

Recent advances in theory, methods and applied knowledge (alongside structural changes in the global economic ecosystem) have presented researchers with challenges in seeking to stay abreast of their fields and navigate new scholarly terrains.

State of the Art in Business Research presents short-form books which provide an expert map to guide readers through new and rapidly evolving areas of research. Each title will provide an overview of the area, a guide to the key literature, and theories and time-saving summaries of how theory interacts with practice.

As a collection, these books provide a library of theoretical and conceptual insights, and exposure to novel research tools and applied knowledge, that aid and facilitate in defining the state of the art, as a foundation stone for a new generation of research.

Network Industries
A Research Overview
Matthias Finger

Strategic Risk Management
A Research Overview
Torben Juul Andersen and Johanna Sax

Management and Organizational History
A Research Overview
Albert J. Mills and Milorad M. Novicevic

For more information about this series, please visit: www.routledge.com/State-of-the-Art-in-Business-Research/book-series/START

Management and Organizational History
A Research Overview

Albert J. Mills and Milorad M. Novicevic

Routledge
Taylor & Francis Group

LONDON AND NEW YORK

First published 2020
by Routledge
4 Park Square, Milton Park, Abingdon, Oxon OX14 4RN

and by Routledge
605 Third Avenue, New York, NY 10017

First issued in paperback 2022

Routledge is an imprint of the Taylor & Francis Group, an informa business

© 2020 Albert J. Mills and Milorad M. Novicevic

Publisher's Note
The publisher has gone to great lengths to ensure the quality of this reprint but
points out that some imperfections in the original copies may be apparent.

British Library Cataloguing-in-Publication Data
A catalogue record for this book is available from the British Library

Library of Congress Cataloging-in-Publication Data
A catalog record has been requested for this book

ISBN 13: 978-1-03-247534-9 (pbk)
ISBN 13: 978-1-138-48589-1 (hbk)
ISBN 13: 978-1-351-04792-0 (ebk)

DOI: 10.4324/9781351047920

Typeset in Times New Roman
by codeMantra

This book is dedicated to *Kaylee Dean*, my Great Granddaughter, who brings a future to my past and *Kristin Williams*, my friend and PhD student, who continually reminds me of the central importance of gender to knowledge of the past.

(Albert J. Mills)

This book is dedicated to Daniel Wren and Art Bedeian, the iconic management historians, who pointed to me the intellectual gravity point from which I could decenter my critical sensemaking of the management's past.

(Milorad M. Novicevic)

Contents

1 History and authorship

Introduction

This book explores key scholarly debates around the inclusion of historical approach and the role of the past in studies of management and organization. The importance of these debates is twofold. On the one hand, they have drawn attention to the dominance of an ahistorical trend within management and organization studies (MOS): a trend that has grown over much of the Cold War era and beyond. On the other hand, the debates have revealed the dominance of an atheoretical thought within the related fields of business, management, and organizational history.

The outcome – far from being conclusive – has been a growing need not only to articulate the role of the past in MOS but also to conceptualize the relationship between history, theory, and the past. If this need were met, we would be able to move beyond giving historical accounts of MOS towards a new and exciting fusion of history and MOS. In this book, we set out the ingredients for such a new approach by reviewing critically a number of key contributions to, what has become known as, the "historic turn in Management and Organization Studies" (Clark & Rowlinson, 2004).

We hope that this journey of revisiting these contributions will expose the reader to many of the central ideas, works, and theorists involved in the link between history and MOS, particularly through debates about the need for an "historic turn." Indeed, we have structured the book in such a way that we use key items of debate around the historic turn to introduce disparate thinkers and events that help us to understand the complex role of the past in management and organizational theory.

In our first chapter, we raise some of the underlying aspects of the production of history. We begin by problematizing the relationship of authorship to historical accounts. We then move on to consideration of the role of narratives before discussing the issue of the historian and (historical) context. This leads us to consideration of history-making and the various agents (or actors) involved in the creation of a sense of history. We conclude with a far-ranging discussion of the role of archives in the production of history.

In Chapter 2, we discuss the influence of starting points on historical accounts and use this discussion to explain and segue into our particular starting point of "the historic turn," around which we introduce various actors and debates in the emerging field of management and organizational history. This sets up our own specific study of the historic turn and its role in the development of the field.

Chapter 3 provides an amodernist account of the development of the historic turn and the implications for study of the production of history. Per the modernist, past events are interpreted as facts.

In Chapter 4, we examine the debates generated by the historic turn and Booth and Rowlinson's (2006) associated manifesto for the development of management and organizational history.

In the final chapter, we revisit the historic turn ten years upon its launching by Clark and Rowlinson (2004) and examine its impact on recent and sharpening debates between positivist and postmodernist historiography. We also examine the extent to which postmodernism brought about by the historic turn has helped to redefine the field of management and organizational history while failing to engender feminist, postcolonial, and decolonial voices.

We hope that our journey through debates around the historic turn will serve as a heuristic to reveal the relationships between communities of practice and the production of historical accounts in management and organizational studies.

Warning: men at work – authorship and historical accounts

Before we take you any further, down the journey mapped in this book, we need to alert you to the hidden obviousness of the book's authorship. Namely, this is a book produced by two men of European heritage who have made their careers in North America. Milorad is from Serbia, gained his PhD at the University of Oklahoma, where he was trained by Daniel Wren, the iconic management historian, and works at the University of Mississippi in the USA. Albert is from the UK, gained his PhD at the University of Durham, and works at Saint Mary's University in Canada. That much is obvious. Less obvious, hidden in fact, is the potential influence of our former and current experiences on how we have come to understand history, the past, management, and organizational studies. Even less obvious is the fact that our engagement with the past, history, and theory is socially constructed in a myriad of ways. Let's explore a few examples. To start with, *being* men is a powerful influence on how we have come to view the world. We have related to people and events over our separate lifetimes through our embodiment. Thus, it can be argued that our relationship to people and events is profoundly gendered. It does not mean that we do not reflect on our embodiment and its impact on what and how we study. It does mean that it is something that we all need to reflect on when making sense of past and extant events. Another point of reflection is on our respective sense of ethnicity. Again, our embodied and cultural experiences have undoubtedly shaped how we have come to view the world. And again, it does not necessarily fix us in a solitary position or viewpoint, but it does challenge us to question our own position in the understanding and construction of historical accounts of eventful and meaningful phenomenon such as feminism, colonialism, and class.

History in translation[1]

Feminist studies of history are plentiful, but few have been taken up in management and organizational history. A good starting point is the work of Sonya Rose (2010), who provides a useful overview of historians' engagement with gender. Also pivotal is the work of Joan W. Scott (2007), who discusses history-writing as critique and argues that gender is historically produced. In terms of management and organization studies a useful example is the work of Joan Acker and Donald van Houten (1974), who re-examined the Hawthorne Studies (Mayo, 1933; Roethlisberger & Dickson, 1939) from a gender lens. Acker and van Houten argue that had the Hawthorne Studies included a focus on gender it would have generated very different results in terms of outcomes for male and female employees and for the way the emergent domain of MOS would have been characterized.

There have also been numerous works published over the past three decades that have critiqued history as the outcome of postcolonial thinking addressing the legacy of colonialism. In particular, the work of Edward Said (1978, 1993) has had a profound influence on management and organizational history, as reflected in the work of Anshuman Prasad (2003). More recently, some management and organizational history scholars (e.g., Faria, Ibarra-Colado, & Guedes, 2010) have been drawn to the work of Walter Mignolo (1991) and other Latin American decolonial scholars.

There have also been a substantial number of historical accounts that focus on the relevance of class for organizational history. The outstanding examples are Stewart Clegg and David Dunkerley's (1980) account of organization, class and control and also Clegg's (1981) work on history as organizational sedimentation and rules.

To return to our discussion of authorship, we are not simply saying that in writing history related to management and organizations we need to be more profoundly reflective, particularly when addressing the themes of feminism, colonialism, and class. We *are* saying not only that but much more. We are contending that the social background of authorship plays a critical role in the development of historical accounts that goes far beyond attempts to reflect on the influence of self on historical facts. As we shall discuss throughout the book, authorship and its context are a critical part of understanding history.

Narrative forms of history

Few historians would ignore the role of narrative in constructing a historical account. Many "factual" (Rowlinson, 2004) historians would nowadays agree that historical facts are given meaning through a narrative account. The facts may be the facts, but they don't actually "speak for themselves" (White, 1984). The historian must decide where to start and end a particular historical account; as well as why a story that emerges from the study provides plausible account. In this way, the historian places importance on his or her craft (Bloch, 1953), the viability and verifiability of archival materials (Webb, Campbell, Schwartz, & Sechrest, 1984), and his or her own ability to carefully emplot (White, 1973) a plausible but real account (Iggers, 1997). At the centre of this approach are the cognitive abilities and training of the historian.

History in translation

Michael (Mick) Rowlinson (2004) distinguishes between three types of historians, each with its own approach and influences. The factual historian, as typified by the work of Alfred Kieser[2] (1994), views "history as a repository of facts" that come to "be known . . . [through] the work of historians" (Rowlinson, 2004, p. 8). The skills of the historian include the ability to select and interpret the facts in contexts of ambiguity and ideological preferences.

The narrative historian, exemplified by the work of Hayden White (1984, 1987),[3] shifts attention away from archival research per se to "the conventions and customs of writing that constitute the craft of history. Here the challenge for the historian is to construct a convincing and plausible narrative of historical events." The "archaeo-genealogical" historian, typified by Foucault (1972), moves the focus of historical examination even further from the other approaches by decentering human motivation and "the conscious human actor" (Rowlinson, 2004, p. 16) to the core of discursive relationships that flow through the thinking of human subjects and of the historian. However, – strangely enough – less attention is given to the thinking of the latter.

In discussing the different historians' approaches to writing history, Rowlinson suggests that there are several influences on the historian that include but go beyond cognitive skills and abilities to reconstruct past reality in a modernist, seemingly objective manner. Narrative writing, for example, is not only influenced by particular skills but also by customs and conventions of writing and by powerful discourses of *being* that shape the way historians think. In the latter case, Rowlinson (2004) seems to suggest that history is not simply written by the historian but that it is also influenced by other social forces that shape such things as who is constituted and legitimized as "the historian" and what is constituted as "history." Indeed, Rowlinson (2004) goes on to question the extent to which the historian in the modernist account is the sole (or primary) constructor of the past, being, as he or she is, trained in "historical methods." Interestingly, postmodernist historians who reject the possibility that the past can be reconstructed arguing that it can only be subjectively constructed, also often privilege the historian in accounts that otherwise set out to reveal the role of discourse, language, and meta-narratives in the construction of history. Callum Brown (2005), for example, is clearly writing to and for historians in his "Postmodernism for Historians." Similarly, Alun Munslow (2010) is focused on fellow historians in his discussion of "the future of history." Both books are peppered with references to the historian and his/her craft. Let's look at some examples, taken at random from each book:

History in translation

Somewhat paradoxically Callum Brown (2005, p. 10) writes:

> Any postmodernist historian is not being a postmodernist all of the time. Like every historian, the postmodernist must conduct empirical research, establishing that events

occurred and the order of them, checking sources that ver-
ify the facts of the case, and making decisions of judgement
(balance of probabilities may be the best term) where abso-
lute certainty is not possible.

Brown's account – although contentious in several ways (do postmodernist historians suspend their postmodernist frame for part
of the time?) – is primarily directing us to the role of the historian
in "history-making" (Kalela, 2012). In the process, he is arguably
ignoring and/or marginalizing the many accompanying acts that
go into "history-making" (Kalela, 2012) prior to/and often without
the engagement of the historian. Here we are thinking of the mul-
titude of people, things, and ideas that go into the making of historical accounts. The Finnish historian Jorma Kalela (2012, p.
xi) provides some perspective on this when he examples the influence
of disciplinary, popular, and public histories on the development
of newer histories. For example, if a historian started out today to
write a history of the "New Deal" (i.e., the policies of the admin-
istrations of the Franklin Delano Roosevelt government), he or
she would find it hard to escape the influence of numerous history
books on the subject (e.g., Hiltzik, 2011), various movies that deal
with the era (e.g., *Mr. Smith Goes to Washington*), the innumerable
artefacts (e.g., bridges, roads, airports) that were constructed by
the Roosevelt Administration (Taylor, 2008), various archival collections (e.g., the Franklin D. Roosevelt Presidential Library and
Museum), and the very *idea* of the New Deal itself. The writing of
history is also, in itself, a pre-existing influence that shapes how
certain accounts are structured (e.g., the use of footnotes), narrated (e.g., told in a particular way and style), and subjected to
ideological and political pressures as well as to the governmental
sources of funding (White, 1973; Zinn, 1990).

In a similar but more complex vein, Munslow (2010) talks about
the challenge of history for the historian thus: "[The] beliefs of the
historian positing – if the historical expression demands it – be
checked against the appropriately contextualized and corrobo-
rated data available." However, he goes on to argue, that "this
logic cannot be extended to the narrative making representational
and culturally expressive level of historical understanding, explanation and meaning creation." Nonetheless, for Munslow, it is the
historian who is seen to carry the burden of this approach, but he
(2010, p. 3) is quick to make clear that the implications "are devas-
tating for history of a particular kind" (i.e., the work of modernist

historians). This leads him to conclude that "historians have to re-think their foundationalist and absolutist dependency on the pre-cepts of common sense, practical realism, induction/inference, the criteria of justification as well as a range of adjacent beliefs that include 'the truth', 'the meaning', 'objectivity', knowable 'agent intentionality' and that ethics and morality can be learned from history" (Munslow, 2010, pp. 76–77).

Yet, as Kalela (2012) seeks to remind us, history is not simply the output of designated (professionally trained) historians.[4] For Kalela (2012, p. x), "history-making is an everyday practice: people continue to make use of their experiences in all sorts of ways." He then goes on to argue that historians "have ignored the purposes and social functions of non-academic histories" (p. x). Part of the reason for this, according to Kalela (2012), is that although only "one strand of history, the discipline has been elevated to a privi-leged position, with the implicit purpose of ruling over other kinds of histories" (p. x). Kalela (2012, p. 53) goes on to state that his "sug-gestion to shift the focus from the historian to practice is intended to have "people addressed as creators of their own histories."

Reflecting on what we have said so far, it has been argued that histo-rians are not the only actors to make history and that there are other actors – some human (e.g., authors), some non-human (e.g., history books), and even some abstract or non-corporeal (e.g., the idea of history itself – see Hartt, 2013) – influence, shape, and produce history.

The historian in context

Before we move on, we will unpack the role of the historian a little further. So far, we have critiqued the view that past events and people are largely narrated as history by the historian; as well as that history narrative is ultimately the outcome of the diligent work of the histo-rian. This critique was never meant to imply that the historian makes the narrative up but, rather, that through his or her training, certain people and events in the past are brought to light through the histori-an's skills in uncovering, recovering, or discovering certain events and people, as well as through the historian's writing abilities.

It is the association between certain people and events in the past, the historian, and the historical account that makes the historian's work so powerful and tends to conflate history with the historian's account of "it." It is this association, according to Kalela (2012), that has served to privilege disciplinary historical accounts over other accounts and other kinds of history. From a modernist perspective,[5] other kinds of history – what Munslow (2010, p. 3) calls "history of a particular kind" – are usually viewed as somehow lessor in value due to the relative or complete lack of methodological training of the author (Kalela, 2012). Or it may be due to the lack of objectivity assessed through source criticism that the (not-professionally trained) author brings to the study of specific past events and/or people (Munslow, 2010). For example, from this perspective, detective novelist Robert Daley's (1980) history of Pan American Airways (Pan Am) was commissioned as a corporate history, whose narrative focused on the heroic role of airline president Juan Trippe. As such, it could be argued to have lost sight of objectivity. Similarly, left-wing journalist Matthew Josephson's (1943) account of Pan Am could be discounted for not being a "real" history because it set out to reveal the misuse of corporate power. This is what Kalela (2012, p. x) is referring to when he contends that this type of objectivist approach ignores "the purposes and social functions of non-academic histories." In the process, socially important and insightful stories can be ignored and devalued.

The espoused objectivist aspect of the professional training of historians has led to the work of certain other historians (e.g., feminists and Marxists) being discounted because of their activist or critical approaches (Lemisch, 1975; Zinn, 1997).

History beyond the historian

The discussion above points to, at the very least, an oblique recognition that history is actually made by a number of people and other (non-human and abstract or non-corporeal) actors (Callon, 1986; Latour, 2005)[6]: more likely than not a large number of actors. The actors may include the historian but not necessarily; where historians are included, they are not necessarily central to the process.

History in translation

As we have seen above, even selected postmodernist historians – Brown (2005) and Munslow (2010), for example – also overly focus on the role of the historian. In fairness, this is, arguably, for three very powerful reasons. First, and the most obvious, is the division of academia into disciplines and the requirement and expectation that academics engage with other academics that will review their work particularly within their own discipline. Second, historians, as noted above, are a powerful group in terms of deciding what history is and who is a legitimate historian. Thus, it makes considerable sense to attempt to influence how this powerful group (and especially future generations of historians) come to rethink their role in history. Third, if we are to accept the idea of history as discursive (Jenkins, 1991; Munslow, 2010), then it makes sense to address concerns/provide insights to key human actors (historians) who are supposedly well positioned to change aspects of the discourse.

However, to return to the work of Kalela (2012), the disciplinary history is but one important kind of history. The other two are public and popular histories. So, this means that other accounts of history and the past are being "written"[7] outside of academia and by individuals, groups, and communities of people that may or may not involve historians and written historical accounts. In recent years, this has led to the study and production of histories through exploration of networks of actors (Durepos & Mills, 2012a, 2012b).

An early version of this approach is that of Durepos, Mills and Helms Mills (2008) who, drawing in part on ANT, sought to understand how a particular history of Pan Am – *An American Saga. Juan Trippe and his Pan Am Empire* (Daley, 1980) – came to be written and what we can learn from the process. Using various archived documents,[8] Durepos and her colleagues were able to trace the production of Daley's history through a series of documented discussions between leading Pan Am Executives (including Company President Juan Trippe, Vice President John Leslie, and company advisor Charles Lindbergh).

These documents revealed a wealth of discussions on the need for a history of the airline, the kind of history it should be, and who should be principally involved in the development and writing of the history. Specific actors involved included Wolfgang Langewiesche, who was initially employed to write the history; a large number of transcripts of interviews that Langewiesche conducted with various company employees; in-house newsletters that produced numerous historical accounts of the airline; a number of historical accounts drafted by John Leslie; and, in this case, the *archive* itself where most of these documents and other artefacts were housed.

Behind closed doors: working in the archives

An archive is arguably a very powerful influence on how historical accounts are written – at least in terms of the professional historian's account. That influence can result from the way how "the archive" is defined and understood (Moore, Salter, Stanley, & Tamboukou, 2017); the epistemological stance of the researcher (Mills & Helms Mills, 2017, 2018); the specific purposes and audiences that the materials were collected for (Yin, 2009); the underlying socio-political pressures behind the establishment of a particular archive (Burton, 2005a); any given archive's "forms of classification, ordering and exclusions" (Ghosh, 2005, p. 28); the discursive character of the times in which the archive was established, and points at which collections are made and at which those collections are being read (Moore et al., 2017); and the extent to which the researcher-archive relationship is caught up in "archive fever" (Derrida, 1995), i.e., psychoanalytical power and identity work (Fritzsche, 2005).[9] This list of potential venues of influence on the production of history is far from comprehensive. These venues are the areas of concern which has generated book-length accounts, see, for example, Burton (2005b) and Moore et al. (2017). Let's briefly review each of the areas of concern we have mentioned above.

Definitional issues

An archive is often defined as a collection of documents and artefacts (Stan, 2010) that are usually housed in a physical location and dedicated to any number of specific people (e.g., Franklin D. Roosevelt Library and Museum), events (e.g., The Imperial War Museum), organizations (e.g., the British Airways Heritage Collection), communities (e.g., the Museum of Humanity), and institutions of national interest (e.g., the Library and Archives Canada and the U.S. National Archives and Records Administration). This type of archives has been referred to as the "canonical version that tends to dominate, the state archive version associated with a disciplining view of what archives and archival research 'ought' to be like" (Moore et al., 2017, p. 2). Yet, as Moore et al. (2017, p. 1) contend, an "archive is a repository of some kind [which can be housed in a building], cardboard-box, photograph album, internet website, or discourse of interconnected ideas such as community heritage and shared memory." How each of these types of archive is accessed and viewed can, arguably, influence the legitimacy of the historical nature of the account, perhaps, encouraging some researchers of the past[10] to avoid the non-canonical forms of archive.[11]

Epistemological stances of the researcher of the past

The influence of the archive on the researcher is not simply a direct one-way street. It involves a relationship that is mediated by the epistemological stance of the researcher. Mills and Helms Mills (2017) differentiate between positivist and postpositivist stances of researchers towards the archive. They contend that the positivist stance is a view of archives "as 'an empirical data corpus' . . . of artifacts and documents that are more-or-less associated with a physical location or "archive"; while a postpositivist stance towards the archive refers to "a set of rules, which at a given period and for a definite society, structure the conditions in and through which knowledge is produced" (Mills & Helms Mills, 2017, p. 96). Rules in this case are sets of practices and expectations (e.g., male only hiring practices based on underlying presumptions about respective male and female abilities), "whose very form and regularities 'govern one's manner of perceiving, judging, imagining, and acting'" (Flynn, 1996, cited in Mills & Helms Mills, p. 96).

While both positivist and postpositivist researchers of the past recognize bias inherent in archival research, the former group is primarily concerned with limitations to objectivity (Elton, 2002; Scott, 1990), the latter group is primarily concerned with recognition of the influence of subjectivism. For the positivist researcher,

> most historical research will therefore involve a detailed critical discussion of the sources utilized in the enquiry in order to ascertain the authenticity, reliability, representativeness, appropriateness and comprehensiveness of the body of sources utilized in the enquiry.
>
> (L'Estrange, 2014, p. 137)

For the postpositivist, on the other hand, "'the archive has neither status or power without an architectural dimension' – that is, a material presence which structures access, imposes its own meanings on the evidence contained therein, and watches over users both literally and figuratively" (Burton, 2005b, p. 9). Further, "archival work is an embodied experience, one shaped as much by national identity, gender, race, and class as by professional training" (Burton, 2005b, p. 9).

Purposes and audiences

From a positivist perspective, Yin (2009, p. 106) warns us that while archives are valuable sources of evidence, the materials they include need to be treated with caution because they were collected with specific purposes and audiences in mind. For example, the British Airways heritage collection originally involved the collection of documents and materials that could be used to provide an ongoing social history of the airline. It was started by former airline employees in the 1980s and served to keep alive the memory of those who had served the airline over its lifetime (Coller, Helms Mills, & Mills, 2016). The audience was, largely, former employees and long-service employees. It would be two decades before the company took a particular interest in the collection, providing limited space to the volunteers involved. Following the subsequent provision of temporary space (in old British Airways' buildings), the collection took on the character of an archive, where employees and researchers could access given materials. The character of the materials changed dramatically in the late 2000s when the company – seeing a corporate advantage in the collection and focusing on the public as its primary audience – moved the archive to its headquarters to serve mostly as a staff museum and collection of marketing materials (Coller et al., 2016). In this way, the socio-politics of the company's archive collection changed. The microhistorian Carlo Ginzburg refers to a different but equally important aspect of the relationship of audience to history. Reflecting on his most famous work – *The Cheese and the Worms (1976)* – Ginzburg was later to state that "the book was published, it was a great success, and then is was taken over by its readers, who have used it for their own purposes." Then, he adds: "Strange though it may seem, I was wholly unprepared for that. It was particularly ironic, as the book is a study of precisely the same process – Menocchio's own adoption of others' writings, the reader's power over the text" (Ginzburg, quoted in Gundersen, 2003, p. 7).

Socio-political pressures

The British Airways case thus provides an example of the socio-politics of archive collections – illustrating how they can change their intended character over time. Burton (2005a, p. 6) sums it up thus:

> archives do not simply arrive or emerge fully formed, nor are they innocent of struggles for power in either their creation or their interpretive applications. . . . [They] come into being in and as history as a result of specific political, cultural and socioeconomic pressures.

One particular area of socio-politics involved the choice of which airline's materials to collect – British Airways, formed in 1974 from the merger of the British Overseas Airways Corporation (BOAC) and British European Airways (BEA); BOAC, formed from a 1939 merger of Imperial Airways Ltd. (IAL) and British Airways Ltd. (BAL); BEA, formed out of BOAC in 1946; IAL's predecessor airlines formed in 1919–1922 and merged in 1924; or all of the 57 airlines officially associated with today's British Airways. The latter choice, established through a series of in-house histories over time, influenced the choice of archival materials as well as the history of the company: for example, the museum is arranged from a series of artefacts that start with a painting of the "airline's first" flight in 1919 and moving relatively seamlessly through 57 successor airlines through to today (Mills, 2002).

Ordering and exclusions

Drawing on Foucauldian theory, ordering refers to a series of conscious and unconscious decisions on what constitutes legitimate evidentiary traces of the past. These decisions become embedded in the processes and structuring of archives – what Burton (2005b, p. 9) refers to as the "architectural dimension" and Gosh (2005, p. 28) conceptualizes as "the logic of the archive"; it is

> a set of complex processes of selection, interpretation, and even creative invention – processes set in motion by, among other things, one's personal encounter with the archive, the history of the archive itself and the pressure of the contemporary moment on one's reading of what is to be found there.
>
> (2005a, p. 8)

The latter touches on the link between ordering and discursivity. The power of ordering is summed up by "Foucault's dictum that history transforms documents into monuments" (Moore et al., 2017, p. 11) and Derrida's view of the archive "as power as reinforced by the valorization of inscription" (Moore et al., 2017, p. 7). Part of the ordering process involves decisions on what is to be included and what is to be excluded.[12] The British Airways Museum, for example, focuses largely on men and machines, privileging pilots, managers, and engineers. Social history, discriminatory practices, and women's role in the development of commercial aviation are largely absent, thus reflecting the socio-politics of the archive.[13]

Discourses, archives, and archive fever

Postmodern researchers of the past focus on discursivity, arguing that history is a meta-discourse (Jenkins, 1991; Munslow, 2010) that encourages a deep-rooted belief in, and need for, making accounts of the past. The story of the making of Pan Am's history (Durepos et al., 2008) is one of many examples, with senior managers and employees striving to have a history of the company written, and the company eventually spending close to a million dollars in current value to have it written (Durepos et al., 2008). From this perspective, part of a dominant discourse in a given era (or "episteme") includes the archive, both as a collection of documents in a physical location and as a set of "interconnected ideas" embedded in established practices (Moore et al., 2017, p. 1). In this view, Pan Am's history illustrates how archival research "is rooted in specific ways of writing and reading the material actualities of an archive and its contents and the resultant ways of shaping the what and the how of these activities" (Moore et al., 2017, p. 9). Yet, the very idea of discursivity means that historians and archivists are not simply disciplined in their discoveries but also interact, and, in the process, change discourses over time. In such cases, archival material is subject to "the pressure of the contemporary moment on one's reading" (Burton, 2005a, p. 8). Indeed, as Moore et al. (2017, p. 3) contend, "the contents of all archives are always read and understood within the present moment." Therefore, it is conceivable that the "archive contains primary sources at the same time it is always a secondary trace of historical discourse" (Moore et al., 2017, p. 11).

History in translation

Despite the ongoing debate on the appropriate epistemological stance to history in recent years, a considerable number of scholars in the area of management and organizational history (MOH) have retained their adherence to the so-called "canonical" versions of the archive (Moore et al., 2017, p. 2). Indeed, one can detect something of a privileging sense of, what is commonly referred to as, "working in the archives." Those who are identified with canonical archive work include Michael (Mick) Rowlinson – Cadbury (1988, 1995); John Hassard – Hawthorne Studies (2012); Alan McKinlay – Bank of Scotland (McKinlay, 2013); Bill Cooke – the Tavistock Institute (Cooke, 2009) and World Bank (Cooke, 2004); Trish Genoe McLaren – Ford Foundation; Gabrielle Durepos – Pan American Airways (Durepos & Mills, 2012b); Adam Rostis – the Red Cross (Rostis, 2015); Albert J. Mills, Jean Helms Mills and colleagues – British Airways (Coller et al., 2016; Mills, 1995), Air Canada (Hartt, Mills, Helms Mills, & Corrigan, 2014), Qantas (Shaffner, Mills, & Helms Mills, 2017) and Pan American Airways (Hartt, Mills, Helms Mills, & Durepos, 2012).

Going beyond the canon and recognizing the move towards socio-materiality in MOS, Mills and Helms Mills (2018) have recently introduced an amodernist (Latour, 1993) approach to archival research, which refers to the study of *relational* links between a range of human, non-human and abstract or non-corporeal actors in the production of knowledge of the past: "With this approach the focus is not so much on developing histories out of available archival materials but rather on analysis of how specific histories come to be developed," and the implications involved in this co-production of history (A. J. Mills & Helms Mills, 2018, p. 36).

While amodernist accounts of the production of (extant) knowledge have been around for almost four decades (see, for example, Callon & Latour, 1981) accounts of "knowledge of the past" are recent developments. these developments were initiated by the work of Durepos et al. (2008) who contend that networks of human, material, and abstract actors strongly influence whether a history comes to be written and how a decision to write a history influences what eventually is produced as history. For example, there was some resistance to a history of Pan Am by Juan Trippe who was concerned that he could be negatively portrayed, as he had been in an earlier leftist history written by Josephson (1944). The eventual outcome was the production of a new history of the airline that is something akin to a corporate history in which Juan Trippe is favorably portrayed as an aviation pioneer and visionary (Durepos et al., 2008).

Other MOS histories that draw on analysis of actor-networks will be discussed in greater depth in the forthcoming chapters of this book, and include Shenhav and Weitz's (2000) use of "constructivist actor-network theory" (p. 375) to make sense of uncertainty in Organization Theory through analyses of "primary data collected from the *American Machinist* and the *Engineering Magazine*" (p. 373); Bruce and Nyland's (2011) study that draws on "Callon and Latour's sociology of 'translation'" (p. 383) to reveal how the Human Relations School wrongly became characterized as a progressive approach to management and organization studies; Myrick, Helms Mills and Mills' (2012) study of how the current history of the Academy of Management came to be written, and Novicevic, Marshall, Humphreys and Seifried's (2018) study that used a "combined ANTi-History/Micro-historical method" to examine James Meredith's leadership during the racial integration of higher education in the United States during the early 1960's "which reveals how social endorsement of Meredith's leadership was accompanied by social contestation."

To summarize, in this chapter we set out to explore various insights into the role of authorship in the production of knowledge of the past. Discussion ranged from the centrality of the historian and his/her professional training, cognitive abilities, and epistemological stance through to the recently decentred notion of the historian as a network of human, non-human, and non-corporeal actors. As we shall demonstrate in subsequent chapters, all these debates loom large in recent developments associated with the historic turn in MOS.

Notes

1 This section, which is repeated at points throughout the book, is written with the intent to uncover and to discuss at some length things that we have raised in the body of the text that are usually in the background of some debates. Feminism, for example, rarely appears in debates about a historic turn in MOS but needs to be foregrounded.

2 This characterization is, in itself, contentious and shaped, among other things by the typology that Rowlinson constructs. Like Gibson Burrell's and Gareth Morgan's (1979) four paradigms of sociological and organizational thought, once you have boxes of typologies to fill you are apt to try to squeeze theorists into them. In the case of Kieser, it can be argued that he doesn't fit neatly into the factualist historian category and could well be located somewhere between the factual and the narrative classification. For example, at some point in his outline he rejects the characterization of historians as "myopic fact-collectors without a method" (Kieser, 1994, p. 612). Nonetheless, he does not go further in addressing those critical issues.

3 There is considerable debate around the character of Hayden White's approach to history. Some have claimed his work as structuralist and others as poststructuralist (Jenkins, 1995). As such, in the latter case, White could also fit in Rowlinson's "archaeo-genealogical" approach.

4 After this point, unless otherwise stated, we will simply refer to "the professionally trained historian" as the historian.

5 In the extant literature the terms "modernist and positivist" are often conflated. While arguably a detailed case can be made for keeping the two terms separate (Johnson & Duberley, 2000), we are using the terms interchangeably. Munslow (2010, p. 3) goes a stage further, referring to "history of a particular kind." Similarly, in debate around postmodernism and poststructuralism some authors make a considerable effort to differentiate the two (Prasad, 2018), while others view them as interchangeable (Bowden, 2018). Again, we take the latter approach.

6 While Latour's Actor-Network Theory (ANT) has not adequately dealt with history and the past it does provide interesting insights into how they might be studied – see Durepos and Mills (2012a) who draw on those insights, along with poststructuralist historiography and the sociology of knowledge, to develop an approach that they call ANTi-History.

7 This is meant metaphorically. Some popular historical accounts, for example, may involve a primarily oral tradition where accounts are passed from

people to people over time (Sarsby, 1988) and/or are eventually written up through the collection of oral accounts (Ellis & McCutcheon, 1996). Other popular accounts may develop through movies – D.W. Griffith's movie *Birth of a Nation* (1915), for example, is said to have influenced the development of the Ku Klux Klan through its racialized imagery and emplotment. See White (2015).

8 Largely from the Pan American World Airways Collection at the Otto Richter Library of the University of Miami.

9 For an interesting book on how national histories are developed, see Furtado (2018).

10 We use this term to avoid the notion that historians are the only people to do archival research.

11 Often time these choices can have interesting and profound outcomes. For example, former Red Cross worker Adam Rostis pursued study of the Biafran War (1968–1971) in the archives of the Museum of the International Red Cross in Geneva. While he had access to a number of documents from that era, he discovered that the archives pertaining to the role of the Red Cross in the Biafran War were not available to the public. Rostis, who identifies his epistemological stance as postcolonial, moved beyond the Red Cross archives to undertake an intensive media search on the War and managed to uncover a wealth of material in the process – concluding that humanitarian organizations, such as the Red Cross, are disciplinary institutions "that dominate and regulate populations through disciplines" (p. 136).

12 See, for example, Gosh (2005) and Decker (2013) on colonial exclusionary practices.

13 In the current BA Museum at the airline's headquarters, the main depiction of female employees is a series of female mannequins dressed in different flight attendants' uniforms. A rare but cursory recognition of the neglect, if not total exclusion, of women is offered by Paul Jarvis – the curator of the collection – whose only comment in his illustrated history of the airline is to say: Following the advent of commercial airlines in Britain "women would not even achieve full voting rights until 1928 and it would take several more decades and another world war before women could begin to take an active part in the operational side of civil aviation" (Jarvis, 2014, p. 30).

2 A starting point
The historic turn

We have chosen to start our exploration of current debates in management and organization history (MOH) with the story of the call for an "historic turn" in management and organization studies (MOS). We do so because much of what has been said in recent debates around this issue provides an outline for understanding different approaches to the past; history; and the related methodological, epistemological, and ontological issues involved in the study of management and organization. We have also chosen this approach to reveal how the historic turn engendered the arguments about the role of narratives (White, 1973, 1987), starting points (Jenkins, 1991), networks (Myrick, Helms Mills, & Mills, 2013), and politics (Zinn, 1990) in the production of history.

To begin with the argument about narratives, Hayden White (1973) contends that it is not facts that shape a historical account but the way those facts are pulled together as a story. White argues that, contrary to common parlance, "facts do not talk for themselves." From an almost unending number of phenomena, some are selected by the historian[1] to constitute the facts of the story and then, through their selection and ordering, those phenomena – constituted as facts – shape the narrative to be told. Along the way, the particular selection of phenomena is often shaped through a political process, a particular focus, and a starting point. To take histories of Pan American Airways (Pan Am), for example, Daley's (1980) *An American Saga: Juan Trippe and his Pan Am Empire* involved a narrative that revolved around the role of airline president Juan Trippe and how he was a "pioneer" of the development and rise of commercial aviation. This set up the starting point of the book with a focus on the life of Juan Trippe: "At the beginning Trippe was both a dreamer and a dare-devil, a youth with mind and heart literally in the clouds [. . .]" (Daley, 1980, p. 6). This was a commissioned history funded by Pan Am and with the approval of

Juan Trippe. On the other hand, Matthew Josephson's (1943) *Empire of the Air* was influenced by his leftist politics, with a focus on "the power politics of the air age" (pp. 3–19) and Juan Trippe's struggle for domination of commercial airways: "The modern empire-builders of the air seem determined to spread their swift lines around the globe in all directions, and act as if they will permit nothing to stop them" (Josephson, 1943, p. xii). A third account of Pan Am's history takes as its starting point the *publication* of Daley's (1980) history, asking how – through what form of networking – did this history get produced (Durepos, Mills, & Helms Mills, 2008):

> We first argue that missing from the current perspectives of crafting company histories is an understanding of how the socio-political context in which the company history is crafted comes to influence the actual story told or knowledge produced about the company history.
>
> (Durepos et al., 2008, p. 63)

History in translation

The starting points and foci of historical accounts have a powerful impact not only on how certain historical management histories are written but also what gets to be narrated as management history. At the end of the 1970s British sociologists Gibson Burrell and Gareth Morgan (1979) made a plea for greater diversity in what was to count as legitimate management and organizational studies (MOS) – arguing that "interpretivist,"[2] "radical structuralist"[3] and "radical humanist"[4] accounts should be considered as legitimate as the "functionalist" (or managerialist) accounts that dominated the field of MOS. Speaking almost exclusively of the latter, Burrell and Morgan (1979, p. 118) contend that "the study of organizations has established itself as an increasingly significant area of social-scientific investigation. . . . [As] a recognised field of study within academic institutions, the study of organisations has a good claim to being regarded as a distinct branch of social science of some importance." They go on to characterize the "field" (p. 118) as objectivist, functionalist, managerialist, "*realist, positivist, determinist,* and *nomothetic*" (Burrell & Morgan, 1979, p. 26 – emphases in the original). In summary, "the 'orthodox approach' to the study of organizations "tends to adopt theories and models of organizational functioning, and to focus on areas of empirical investigation, that are highly oriented towards managerial conceptions of organizations, managerial priorities and problems, and managerial concerns for practical outcomes" (Burrell & Morgan, 1979, p. 118).

Here we see a call for the expansion of "the field" to include different foci (e.g., community-oriented concerns); ontological orientation (i.e., subjectivist); epistemological roots (e.g., antipositivism); and methodologies (e.g., ideographic approaches). In short, it was being argued that inclusion in the field of MOS depended on making the correct intellectual and political choices, choices that were influencing who or what was considered legitimate aspects and voices of the field and who or what was considered legitimate histories of management and organization studies.

To the latter point, while Burrell and Morgan referred to each of the paradigms as historically constituted intellectual communities they had little to say on the role of each paradigm in developing histories of the field (Mills, 1988). Yet, had they done so, they may have noted that legitimate histories of the field (George, 1968, 1972; Urwick, 1938; Urwick & Brech, 1944, 1957a, 1957b, 1957c; Wren, 1972, 1979) not only mirrored the largely functionalist paradigm in its managerialist and factualist accounts but also served as a powerful agent in the legitimization of the field itself. Instead, Burrell and Morgan (1979), somewhat paradoxically, drew on factualist, managerialist histories of the field to reveal some of the shortcomings of the functionalist paradigm. In other words, they treated managerialist accounts of the past as history. In a similar way, five years earlier, Harry Braverman (1974) had drawn on managerialist accounts of the past to reveal the problems of Taylorism as an ideology. In the year following Burrell and Morgan's (1979) work on paradigms, Stewart Clegg and David Dunkerley (1980) published a radical structuralist account of managing and organizing that pointed to the role of Marxist theory and historical materialism in legitimizing managerialist theory.

Less paradoxically, Burrell and Morgan reproduced an absence or "neglect" (Hearn & Parkin, 1983) of gender theory and feminist communities from their construction of different paradigmatic perspectives (Mills, 1988).[5] Yet, five years earlier Acker and Van Houten's (1974) feminist critique of the field aimed straight at the neglect of gender in so-called classic historical studies of MOS, specifically the Hawthorne Studies and Michel Crozier's study of French bureaucracies. Meanwhile, following the publication of *Sociological Paradigms*, Jeff Hearn and Wendy Parkin (1983) produced a sweeping critique by revealing the range and depth of feminist research that could be found (located in) each of four major paradigms.

Meantime, in addition to the emerging feminist paradigm, other ontological challenges (Donaldson, 1985)[6] were also in the making, including poststructuralism (Foucault, 1970), postmodernism (Lyotard, 1979), postcolonialism (Said, 1978), and amodernist approaches (Latour & Woolgar, 1979). Each in its own way was to influence the direction and understanding of history in the field of MOH.[7]

In summary, it can be argued that Burrell and Morgan's (1979) claim of a schism in MOS is important to subsequent debates on the role of history in MOS. To begin with, it revealed the potential for different onto-epistemological approaches to the construction of MOS as an important field of enquiry. Secondly, it opened the door to yet other paradigms and communities of thought, including feminism (Hearn and Parkin, 1983), postmodernism (Boje, Gephart, & Thachenkery, 1986); postcolonialism (Prasad, 2002), amodernism (Hunter & Swan, 2007), etc. Third, it exacerbated the potential ontological and epistemological differences between accounts of the past and those of the present. Making it increasingly difficult over subsequent years to match realist accounts of the past with discursive notions of extant meanings. Yet, as we will see below, it took time before the disconnect between the ontological-epistemological differences between the past and history were fully appreciated (Munslow, 2015).

As has been argued elsewhere (Mills & Helms Mills, 2011, 2018), one's philosophical or paradigmatic stance is a crucial starting point that will shape what he or she looks for (e.g., "the waning of collectivity" – Samuel, 2006, pp. 3–17), and how he or she looks for it (e.g., through the method of historical materialism). In terms of broad-brush strokes, one's starting point may be *modernist* (i.e., seeking historical truth through the gathering of factual material – what Rowlinson, 2004, refers to as factual accounts), *postmodernist* (i.e., seeking clues to changing discursive views over time – what Rowlinson refers to as Archaeo-Genealogical approaches), and *amodernist* (i.e., searching for networks of activities associated with the production of particular histories – see Durepos and Mills, 2012a).

Such philosophical starting points are accompanied by other starting points, in particular, a point in time (e.g., the late 19th century), a particular geographic space (e.g., the USA), an event (e.g., the development of scientific management), a specific person (e.g., Frederick Taylor), and community (e.g., the Taylor Society). These choices affect what becomes important to the narrative.

History in translation

A number of accounts of the starting point of management and organization studies designate Frederick Taylor as "the father" of modern management (Baird, Post, & Mahon, 1990; Beach, 1985; Davis & Newstrom, 1985). In so doing they root MOS in managerial perspectives linked to bottom-line concerns of profit, efficiency, growth, and effectiveness. This, in turn, led to the work of Taylor and some of his contemporaries being classified as a school of thought – namely *scientific management* (Koontz, 1961). However, the depiction of scientific management almost exclusively came to be associated with the managerialist aspects of the approach, to the exclusion of leftist and feminist Taylorites (Nyland & Heenan, 2005; Nyland & Rix, 2000; Phipps, 2011; Rose, 1978). In the process several leading female theorists – including Mary van Kleeck, Mary Parker Follett, Lillian Gilbreth, and Mary Barnett Gilson – were neglected and marginalized in histories of modern management (Ansell, 2009; Graham, 1996; Novicevic, Harvey, Buckley, Wren, & Pena, 2007; Nyland & Heenan, 2005; Phipps, 2011; Tancred-Sheriff & Campbell, 1992). The socially constructed notion of "schools of thought" was further compounded as management theorists and historians sought out other schools of thought – among the various theories and studies of organization and management – that could be seen to follow, emerge from, or as a reaction to scientific management (Novicevic, Jones, & Carrahar, 2015).

The choice of the newer school of thought fell to what eventually became known as the Human Relations School and its association with a series of experiments at the Hawthorne Works of the General Electric company in the period from the mid-1920s to the mid-1930s (M. Rose, 1978). The impression is given of a group of management researchers (largely from Harvard Business School but also, in some accounts, sociologists from the University of Chicago – see Wren, 1979) who were making an impact on the emerging field of management through their focus on the "human problems of work" (Mayo, 1933). Certainly a series of monographs developed out of the work at the time and included Mayo's (1933) *The Human Problems of an Industrial Civilization*, Whitehead's (1938) *The Industrial Worker*, and Roethlisberger and Dickson's (1939) *Management and the Worker*. However, there is scant evidence that management researchers were paying much attention to this "school" – at least not until well into the first two decades of the post-WWII era. Surveys of US management textbooks of the era (1925–1945), for example, reveal little or no references to "the Hawthorne Studies," and even those that do focus on technical rather than sociological issues (Foster, Mills, & Weatherbee, 2014).

The various choices that were made to ground the field of management in the work of Taylor and the parallel exclusion of feminists and leftists have arguably led to a characterization of the field that is largely focused on managerialist (Cooke, 1999), masculinist (Hearn, Sheppard, Tancred-Sheriff, & Burrell, 1989), and colonialist (Cooke, 2003a, 2004) concerns. These foci have helped to shape histories of the field, which in turn have, reinforced existing notions of the field. To take the issue of gender as an example. For the longest time Mary Parker Follett was excluded from numerous histories of the management field (Phipps, 2011; Tancred-Sheriff & Campbell, 1992). That is one level of problem. A second level of problem has seen feminist researchers trying to insert Parker Follett (and other female theorist) into existing managerialist histories, claiming that she was the forerunner of the Human Relations School (Graham, 1996). Other feminists have argued that this process, although important in terms of revealing women's contribution to managing and organizing, has shaped Parker Follett's work through existing masculinist and managerialist lenses (Calás & Smircich, 1996). As has been argued elsewhere, focus on two sites of enquiry – Taylor's study at Bethlehem Steel (around 5,000 employees) and the work of Mayo and his colleagues at the Hawthorne works (30,000 employees) are both overshadowed in scope by Franklin D. Roosevelt's New Deal administration that set out, using a range of unique activities and policies, to put millions of people to work (Hiltzik, 2011; Taylor, 2008). Yet, even though the Hawthorne Studies were on-going alongside the New Deal, management histories have tended to largely ignore the New Deal and the potential lessons for managing and organizing (Foster et al., 2014; Mills, Weatherbee, Foster, & Helms Mills, 2015), including the work of Frances Perkins (Williams & Mills, 2017), Hallie Flanagan (Williams & Mills, 2018), Mary van Kleeck (Nyland & Rix, 2000) and other various other women.[8]

Scientific Management and the work of Frederick Taylor have not been the only starting points. Some accounts place Robert Owen at the forefront of the development of management theory (see, for example, Urwick & Brech, 1957a). This is somewhat curious as Owen is usually associated with developing the idea of co-operatives in opposition to capitalist versions of ownership and control (Humphreys et al., 2016). The way that Urwick and Brech deal with that somewhat contradictory idea is to argue that Owen's concern with employee welfare made him the "pioneer of personal management" (Urwick & Brech, 1957a, pp. 40–59). In other cases Harrington Emerson is sometimes placed as the forerunner of Taylor in developing scientific management, sometimes as a contemporary of Taylor and sometimes a disciple of Taylor (Wren, 1979).

In this chapter we have (i) discussed the influence of starting points on historical accounts; (ii) prepared the reader to be aware of the underlying starting point of our next chapter, namely the "historic call"; and (iii) set up our extended example to reveal how starting points work in action, in other words, an applied account of the development of the past by management and organizational historians.

Notes

1 That is not to suggest that the historian is the only actor to select and order "the facts." As we have argued in Chapter 1, certain phenomena may already be designated facts and ordered accordingly by networks of actors that subsequently enroll the historian. For example, the decision that documents should be digitized for public access precedes the engagement of the historian.

2 This paradigm was based on approaches that were largely seen as rooted in phenomenological philosophy:

> The interpretive paradigm embraces a wide range of philosophical and sociological thought which shares the common characteristic of attempting to understand and explain the social world primarily from the point of view of the actors directly involved in the social process. . . . [The] ultimate reality of the universe lies in 'spirit' or 'idea' rather than in the data of sense perception.
>
> (Burrell & Morgan, 1979, p. 227)

Here Burrell and Morgan (1979) include the works of Schutz (1978), Gadamer (1976), and Garfinkel (1967) as exemplars of this approach.

3 This paradigm refers, largely, to various Marxist and leftist Weberian accounts (Althusser, 1970; Gramsci, 1978; Marx, 1999).

4 Based largely on leftist existentialist accounts (for example, Sartre, 1957), Burrell and Morgan (1979, p. 279) distinguish between interpretivism and radical humanism thus:

> The interpretive and radical humanist paradigms are both founded on the notion that the individual creates the world in which he (sic) lives. But, whereas the interpretive theorists are content to understand the nature of this process, the radical humanists subject it to critique, focusing on what they regard as the essentially alienated state of man (sic).

Exemplars here include the early work of Marx (1844/1967), "French existentialism" (e.g., Sartre, 1948), and "Critical theory" (e.g., Marcuse, 1964).

5 For Gareth Morgan's response to the absence of gender from the Paradigms book see Mills, (1988).

By the time of publication of Burrell and Morgan's 1979 book Joan Acker and Donald van Houten's article (1974) on the "sex structuring of organizations" had appeared in the *Administrative Sciences Quarterly*, Rosabeth Moss Kanter's (1977) *Men and Women of the Corporation* was in print, and Janet Wolff's (1977) *Women in Organizations* appeared in Clegg and Dunkerley's (1977) edited book on *Critical Issues in Organizations*.

6 We have used the word "challenges" here to reflect some high-profile responses to Burrell and Morgan's (1979) call for a multi-paradigmatic approach to the field of Organization Theory: in particular Lex Donaldson's (1986) "defence of Organization Theory" and his call to resist the intrusion of anti-positivist and other radical theories into the field. For Donaldson the "orthodox approach" (see above) was the only legitimate contribution to theories of organization. More recently Donaldson's fellow Australian Bradley Bowden (2018) has launched a similar attack on postmodern and amodern approaches to history in MOH, writing: "[The book] seeks to defend what once needed no defence: the modern world with its universities, its immense wealth, and its deeply ingrained traditions of democracy and respect for individual rights" (p.vi). More on this later!

7 For the influence of Burrell and Morgan's (1979) book see Corman and Poole (2000); Hassard (1991); Hassard and Wolfram Cox (2013); Mills, Helms Mills, Bratton and Foreshaw (2007); Reed (1990); Willmott (1993).

8 Interestingly enough, for those interested in "schools of thought," Mary Parker Follett and several leading members of the New Deal, including Perkins, Flanagan, van Kleeck, Harry Hopkins and Harold Ickes, were trained and involved in Social Work – suggesting a possible Social Work School of Management to be explored!

3   Not a history

The call for a historic turn in management and organizational studies

In many ways the call for a historic turn in management and organization studies (MOS) is a curious starting point. In one regard it can be argued that there was more than one call but, in another regard, it can be argued that there were no actual calls. It can also be argued that the call was needed because mainstream MOS has become increasingly ahistorical (Burrell & Morgan, 1979). However, it can also be argued that history has always been a part of MOS (Wren & Bedeian, 2009).

For us, drawing on an amodernist perspective (Durepos, 2015), the call for a historic turn (hereafter referred to as "the call") in MOS provides an opportunity to see how an idea (i.e., "the call") is developed, is mobilized (i.e., disseminated), and gains a sense of legitimacy (i.e., how something is deemed worthy of reproduction). It also provides a way of introducing several theories, approaches to history and theorists. As such, much of what we will say in the rest of this short book will be more-or-less limited to those people, things, and events that we associated with "the call." In other words, we will be presenting a slice of the broader discussions around history and MOS but then only a small part of it. However, we hope that our selection of people, things, and events are sufficient to provide a signpost to an important aspect of the debate around the role of history in MOS.

There is considerable agreement that there was a call for a historic turn in MOS somewhere between the early 1990s and the early part of the 21st century (Mills, Suddaby, Foster, & Durepos, 2016). This is in large part due to an article by Clark and Rowlinson (2004) that primarily focuses on the "treatment of history in organization studies" but in the process asks the question whether their observations can be characterized as being "Toward an 'historic turn' in business?"

Clark and Rowlinson (2004) suggest that there have been set of four significant calls for a historic turn that preceded their own. Here they cite the work of Mayer Zald (1993), Alfred Kieser (1994), Roy Jacques (1996), and Gibson Burrell (1997), commenting that this set signals "an increasing call for an historical perspective in organization studies" (Clark & Rowlinson, p. 331). Despite their scepticism about the characterization of history across the past debate, Clark and Rowlinson (2004, p. 331) add their voices to the call, arguing that "the term 'historic turn' may prove useful in marshalling support for calls for more history, and a different approach to history." In other words, the idea of a historic turn can be a useful heuristic for encouraging further interest in the use of history in MOS but also a precursor to opening debate around the character of the study of history. The latter issue would loom larger in a future article by Booth and Rowlinson (2006).

In 2006, several related developments may have provided some evidence that the historic turn was indeed underway. At the end of 2005 a Special Issue of *Management Decision* signalled a revival, or relaunching, of the *Journal of Management History* (*JMH*), following a hiatus of six years when it was incorporated under *Management Decision*. The theme of the Special Issue was "Management history: absorbing the past to understand the present and inform the future,"[1] under the editorship of David Lamond. Although it does not refer to the historic turn, the focus of Lamond's (2005) guest editorial was "On the value of management history," stating that the paper's purpose "is to consider the value of management history as a contributor to the development of the theory and practice of management" (p. 1273). A few months later in 2006 the revived *JMH* was published. That same year *Human Relations* published a Special Issue on "Management as a Cold War phenomenon?" Edited by Elizabeth Kelley, Albert Mills, and Bill Cooke, the issue set out to draw attention to the socio-political contexts in which management histories are produced. Towards the end of 2006 a new journal – *Management & Organization History* (*M&OH*) – appeared alongside *JMH*, edited by Charles Booth, with co-editors Mick Rowlinson and Roy Jacques.[2] The opening line of the lead article, co-authored by Booth and Rowlinson (2006, p. 6), stated clearly that "Our starting point is the 'historic turn' that is arguably taking place in management and organization theory" (Clark and Rowlinson, 2004). They go on to characterize the phenomenon as "akin to that which has transformed other branches of the social sciences and humanities" (p. 6). As we shall discuss later, much of the rest of the article focused on issues of the characterization, theorization, methods of analysis, and styles of writing history.

One good turn . . .

Following Clark and Rowlinson's (2004) scepticism of the treatment of history in MOS, we take a step back to analyse the authors they draw on as exemplars of the call for a historic turn – Mayer Zald, Alfred Kieser, Roy Jacques, and Gibson Burrell.[3]

Mayer Zald

The title of Zald's 1993 article – "Organization Studies as a Scientific and Humanistic Enterprise" – provides a better sense of the scope of his argument, an argument that goes beyond a discussion of history and organization studies. Zald's central argument is that "organization studies must be reconfigured as science *and* humanities" (p. 513). His argument rests on both an ethical and a methodological stances. In terms of the former, Zald (1993, p. 514) proposes an "'enlightenment' model" – not "a model presupposing a singular canon, a linear organization of progress and rationality [but of] a model of an applied discipline in which the goal is education for public and civic participation, not necessarily for specific problem solving" (p. 514). Later, Zald (1993, p. 518), in a more critical mode, states: "Organizations are not only instruments for creating products and profits. They are instruments of power and domination. They are major sources of the individual's sense of wholeness and participation or alienation and worthlessness" (p. 518). It is against the background of discussion about methodology that the issue of history comes to the fore, as part of an overall process of repositioning the field of organization studies. Here he makes six key points:

1   Organization studies – "in the rush to be scientific" (p. 514) – is or has become detached from "the philosophical, philological, historical and hermeneutic traditions" (ibid.).
2   Social science theories appear to assume that their findings "will apply to behaviour in all societies at all times" (p. 515).
3   The context in which theories produced is rooted in "concrete historical and civilizational events and trends" (p. 515).
4   The "humanistic disciplines render behaviour in *specific time and societal contexts* . . . [rather than] as a generalized measurement of distance between events" (p. 518, our emphasis).
5   "Most history eschews the strong form of the positivist programme: No universal generalizations; explicit evaluative standpoints based on the historians' identification with the rise and fall

of national and cultural interests or of western social values; a concern for literary style in presentation; the use of literary tropes and devices to render the dramatic structure imposed on the flow of events" (p. 518).

6   What the field of organization studies needs for a reconfiguration is "the development of a historically informed organizational theory, semiotics and the close reading of texts, the use of rhetoric for substantive analysis and meta-methodological reflection, and narrative analysis and policy evaluation."

Observations

Our first observation is that Zald was profoundly concerned with the development of a more humanistic approach to organization studies, in which history played an important part, underwritten by a critical ethical stance and alongside humanist forms of method and writing styles. As such, it was more than a call for a historic turn *in* MOS but rather a call for a radical change in the ethical underpinnings and preferred methodological approaches of the study of organizations. Arguably, it was a call for a shift from a behavioural to a more sociological character of the field. In short, Zald seems to envision a radically changed field of organization studies, in which history alongside other methods transforms the very character of organization studies. We note here that history (as study of the past) is conflated with (historical) methods for studying the past.

Our second observation is that nowhere does Zald define history. If anything, we glimpse it through the ways he examples history (e.g., as contextual phenomena – see points 3 and 4 above) and how he refers to its use (e.g., as the character of a specific period in time – see point 3). We learn that historical accounts produce the opposite of universalist and presentist findings (see points 2 and 5 above). Instead we glimpse the idea of history as a series of embedded ideas and influences that constitute different contexts in different time periods (points 3–5). We also come to view history through the methods used in the humanities that include forms of narrative analysis, hermeneutics, and (in a circular way) history itself. Finally, and again as part of the humanities, we come to understand history through the way its accounts are presented (see point 5). Thus, without a clear understanding of history (and its relation to the past) it is difficult to say what is meant by the term "historically informed organizational theory" (see point 6) except to suggest that organization studies should take into account the roots and traces of its past when outlining research findings.

Our third observation is that the debate engendered by Zald is largely focused on the field of organization studies as constituted through a Western perspective. In fairness to Zald, in three important passages he signals the influence of Western thought and context on the construction of the field. Two of his observations are highlighted above (points 3 and 5). The third is as follows:

> A theory of social stratification and social change drawn from the experience of Western Europe offers limited application to India; a theory based on the emergence of state bureaucracies in the West does not map onto the Incas of the Catholic Church in the sixth century.
>
> (p. 515)

Nonetheless, the debate lies within the parameters of Western concerns with organization studies, with its focus on debates largely within the USA and, to a lesser extent, the UK (Clegg, Ibarra Colado, & Bueno-Rodriques, 1999; Cooke, 2003b; Ibarra-Colado, Faria, & Lucia Guedes, 2010).

Alfred Kieser

In the year when Zald's (1993) article appeared, Alfred Kieser gave a talk at the European Group for Organization Studies (EGOS) meeting in Paris on "the importance of historical analysis of organizations and the relative absence of this perspective in contemporary organizational science" (Frost, 1994, p. 608). According to Peter Frost, an Associate Editor of the journal *Organization Science*, Arie Lewin – the journal's Editor-in-Chief – was in the audience and invited Kieser to submit a paper. Kieser agreed and Peter Frost was assigned to work with Kieser to "shape the manuscript" (Frost, 1994, p. 608). The result was "Why organizational theory needs historical analyses – And how this should be performed," published in 1994.

From the title onwards this was a strong argument for including historical analysis in theorizing studies of organizations. He begins by contending that in contrast to previous generations of sociologists of organization who "took history very seriously," current interest has vanished; such research is now "extremely rare" (p. 609). He then proceeds to make four major arguments in favour of historical analysis:

1 In order to understand contemporary institutions it is important to know something of their historical development (Kieser, 1994, p. 609).[4]

2   Through historical analysis we can reduce the ideological biases that are embedded in current "'fashionable' trends in organization theory and practice" (p. 610).

3   Through historical analyses we can "interpret existing organizational structures not as determined by [objective] laws but as a result of decisions in past choice opportunities, whether intentional or implicit" (p. 611).

4   "By confronting theories of organizational changes with historical development, these theories can be subjected to a more radical test than they have to pass when merely being confronted with data on short-run changes" (p. 612).

Observations

First, and foremost, we again note that history is nowhere defined in the article. Kieser's numerous references to history seem to exemplify Munslow's (2010) argument that the past and history are often conflated. Thus, there are various references that evoke the past as if it is history and vice versa. For example, Kieser refers to such things as "the history of" (p. 609), "back in history" (p. 610), "found in history" (p. 610), and "a look into history" (p. 610). Thus, while there is a debate about the use of history in organization theory there is not a debate about what history is (see point 1 above). Throughout the article history is very much a taken-for-granted thing that constitutes and infuses contexts and their *discoverable* influences.

The second observation is that, unlike Zald, Keiser was focused not so much on "reconfiguring" organization studies through a move to integrate organization theory and history but rather to improve the field with the infusion of historical analyses. Thus, while Zald aimed at developing a new form of historically informed, humanistic, organization theory, Kieser argued for history as a useful methodology for organization studies to explore past organizational events underlying extant processes (see points 1–3). In that regard, Kieser makes an interesting point about the relationship between the past and present (see points 1–3) but because neither is theorized (in particular the relationship of the past to history) its significance is lost.

The third and related observation is that Kieser's view of history was itself rooted in a singular account, namely, implying the possibility of a real or "actual history" (Rowlinson, 2004, p.9). This is outlined clearly in point 4 above. Our observation is similar to the observation by Rowlinson (2004) who characterizes Kieser's approach as "factual" (see Chapter 1).[5]

The fourth observation is that, minus a changing perspective on the ethical stance of organization theory, the unfolding debate very much reflected the gendered tone of the field at that time: basically gender was either ignored or "neglected" (Hearn & Parkin, 1983; Mills & Tancred, 1992). Likewise, the argumentation was framed by debates around Western social values (Cooke, 2004).[6]

The Kieser-Goldman debate

Having invited Alfred Kieser to submit a paper to *Organizational Science*, Peter Frost invited Paul Goldman "to read and respond to Kieser's paper" (Frost, 1994, p. 608). According to Frost, Goldman – "noted for his work in the late 1970s on the labour process" – cautions against an uncritical embracing of history as an explanation of organizational structure, processes, and outcomes" (p. 608).

Goldman agrees with Kieser that the field of organization studies has largely become ahistorical. However, rather than arguing for more historical analysis in the field, Goldman takes it as a point of departure for exploring how the field "has evolved in a fashion that discounts the past" (p. 621). He begins with a critique of Kieser's characterization and application of history, arguing that Kieser "uses history and culture almost interchangeably" (p. 621). He then goes on to discount Keiser's view of history as value free, arguing that

> historical analysis cannot truly free us from ideology . . . [and] may add to our own contemporary biases those distortions that originate either from creators of documents and artifacts we use from those persons who subsequently collect, catalog, or interpret them.
>
> (p. 621)

Goldman notes that Kieser raises but does not resolve the question of "whether the contextual 'rules of the game are fixed or mutable" (p. 621). Finally, he criticizes Kieser's example of studying a phenomenon in time (the putting out system) as a starting point and studying it forward in time "rather than selecting one that has emerged more recently and working *that* back through time" (p. 623, Goldman's emphasis). In terms of pinpointing barriers to the inclusion of history in organization studies, Goldman lists three main points: (i) the field of "organizational science" is theoretically underdeveloped, lacking agreed upon propositions about how organizations work, (ii) the field has very much become an applied area of study that "reinforces mainstream thinking" (p. 623), and (iii) the majority of PhD training and research in the USA occurs in management departments.

Observations

Our first observation is that yet again neither Kieser nor Goldman seem to be defining either history or the past or the relationship between the two. To a substantial extent, Goldman literally takes Kieser at his word, debating with him over something that is far from clear and which lacks a common definition. At best, Goldman makes one reference to "the past" that he seems to equate with history (p. 621).

Our second observation is the similarity between Goldman and Zald in highlighting the character of organization theory as a mitigating factor in the gap between history and organization studies. While Zald sees history as a way to strengthen the critically ethical stance of organization studies, Goldman sees history as a generally outmoded source of data and form of analysis for a theoretically underdeveloped field that is moving "towards middle range theory, towards sometimes simplistic metaphor, and towards heuristic rather than grand theoretical analysis" (p. 622). If nothing else this suggests that any attempt to encourage a historic turn in organization theory requires that we ask, "What is history?" And, "What is organization theory?" We shall return to this later.

Our third observation returns us to the Western framework of the debate. If anything, Kieser's (1994) euro-centric argument[7] is exacerbated by the inclusion of Paul Goldman from the University of Oregon, whose argument tends to view both history and organization studies as two universal disciplines.

Our fourth observation returns to the issue of gender. In his acknowledgements, Goldman (1994, p. 623) includes thanks to his University of Oregon colleague Donald van Houten for providing "helpful feedback on an earlier draft of (his) commentary." Interestingly, van Houten co-authored with Joan Acker, a leading feminist organizational theorist, a classic revisiting of the Hawthorne Studies from a gender perspective (Acker & van Houten, 1974). We do not know what van Houten advised but, if Goldman took his advice, but we expected to read more than the following aspect of the commentary:

> There has been a modest, if growing, research effort on gender issues *inside* organizations, and this has often been atheoretical, emphasising management issues created by the new demography

and new consciousness *about* women, rather than how gender may serve as a construct that transcends organizational boundaries.

(p. 623, our emphasis)

We would note that Goldman was writing this commentary 20 years after the publication of Acker and van Houten's study (1974) and of numerous other feminist studies and theories of organization.[8]

History in translation

Twenty years after Alfred Kieser's call for a historically informed organisation theory, he publically reflected on his original argument. His account, published in 2015 (see Kieser, 2015), was somewhat surprising to many in the field of management and organizational history. Writing a "comment on [his] perception of the impact of [his] essay on the need for historical analyses in organization studies" (p. 47), Kieser makes the following points.

First, he contends that Clark and Rowlinson (2004, p. 346) were correct in their assessment that

> an historic turn would entail questioning the scientifistic rhetoric of organizational studies, an approach to the past as process and context, and not merely as a variable . . . However, we maintain that . . . *the scientistic analytic schemas of organization studies are resistant to an historic turn.*
>
> (quoted in Kieser, 2015, p. 47, our emphasis)

Kieser then summarises in a curt manner, namely: "A historical turn is still not identifiable and probably never will be (2005, p. 47). He goes on to add that, his "impression today is that [he] greatly overrated the possibilities of historical analyses within organization studies" (p. 47).

By way of explanation, he returns to the four major arguments that he made in his 1994 article. Thus, in regard to point 1, "culture-specific historical analyses," he contends that "studies that compare organizations across different national cultures have died out" (p. 46). In regard to ideology, Kieser argues that there is resistance to the characterization of scientific research as ideology to the point where the claim to be doing scientific research means that, logically it can't be ideological: "Tautological reasoning caused by ideology can serve as a shield against the critique of being ideological . . . [Thus, if] science is entrapped in ideology, historical studies are unable to mediate . . ." (p. 48). Moving on to his third original point, Kieser contends that "In principle it still seems a good approach to study organizations that decided against the current dominant fashion" (p. 48) but, for reasons that are not particularly clear, he doubts if such examples are easy to find any more. Finally, he comments on the probability of developing testable theories: "I must confess that 20 years ago, I was naïve to assume that the quality of theories could be assessed by the quality of the results that they produce. However, the only test is the relation of peers who like certain results to those who do not" (p. 48).

He concludes the commentary with a somewhat resigned yet whimsical response:

> Looking back, I conclude that the problems that I listed 20 years ago as challenges for historical analyses seem to have disappeared. Nevertheless, if organization studies did not make a historical turn, a very lively discourse on the use of historical studies in organizational analyses developed in a historically oriented sub-community on the basis of witty article, foundations of scholarly journals, and editions of prudent handbooks.
>
> (p. 48)

We sincerely hope that Alfred is able to include this book among the prudent!

Gibson Burrell and Roy Jacques

In searching for examples of calls for "more history in organization studies" Clark and Rowlinson (2004, p. 332) included two books – *Pandemonium* by Gibson Burrell (1997) and *Manufacturing the Employee* by Roy Jacques (1996). Burrell, like Zald (1993), is cited as questioning the "separation of business disciplines from the social sciences and humanities, especially sociology and history" (Clark & Rowlinson, 2004, p. 333). Jacques, meantime, is cited as making a case "for the practical value of historical perspective" and concluding that "an historical perspective will be 'invaluable,' indeed unavoidable, if organisation studies is expected to provide a critically reflective vision of the good society, or inform debate between alternative visions of that society" (Jacques, 1996, p. 9, cited in Clark & Rowlinson, 2004, p. 333).

Observations

While the works of Burrell and Jacques are interesting studies that deal with history and organization studies, we would argue that they are exemplars of a different kind. As Clark and Rowlinson (2004) recognize, Burrell and Jacques are undertaking analyses from a

Foucauldian perspective: "Jacques and Burrell in particular are advocates of an historical orientation derived from Foucault, the French philosopher-cum-historian" (Clark & Rowlinson, 2004, p. 333). In the process, Burrell and Jacques are not so much arguing for a "reconfiguration" of organization studies or for a "reintegration" of history and organization studies but, rather, undertaking/performing Foucauldian analysis, which simultaneously draws on discursive history as a corollary of the discursive study of organizations. This point is more clearly expressed in Rowlinson (2004), where he focuses on Foucauldian (or "archaeo-genealogical") analyses as one of three major "variants" of historical perspectives in organization studies (p.8).

We note that the debate was still continuing in a largely Western framework but was beginning to open up with the contribution of Foucauldian analysis to the emergent postcolonial theorization of history and organization studies (Calás, 1992; Calás & Smircich, 2005; Prasad, 1997, 2003; Said, 1978, 1993).

In terms of gender, Jacques (1996) very much takes this on board. For example, reflecting on the "simplistic" argument for dealing with workplace discrimination by adding women, Jacques argues that this

> fails to recognize that women in the workplace have achieved organizational prominence to the degree that they have been able to work within the norms of that organization . . . [Thus, we need to take] a broader historical perspective.
>
> (Jacques, p. 178)

While Burrell (1997) has less to say about gender his views on this are better served by inclusion of his earlier work on "Sex and Organizational Analysis" where he argues that "sexuality is not a given; it is a social construction . . . Sexuality is thus an historic construct which needs to be understood historically"[9] (Burrell, 1984, p. 97).

The interregnum

The 2004 article by Peter Clark and Mick Rowlinson is often viewed as the foundation (or consolidating) call for history in organization studies. This is seemingly the opinion of Mick Rowlinson. However, as we shall see below, numerous other commentaries example the later article by Booth and Rowlinson (2006) as the starting point of the call.

In 2004, at least three companion pieces to the Clark and Rowlinson (2004) article were published: one was authored by Rowlinson (2004), a second by Usdiken and Kieser (2004), and a third by Leblebici and Shah (2004). All three focus on history and organization studies and arguably should be read alongside the Clark and Rowlinson (2004) article. Interestingly enough three of these four works (viz. Rowlinson, Usdiken and Kieser, and Leblebici and Shah) appeared in the same issue of *Business History*.[10]

Perhaps somewhat ironic, the article by Usdiken and Kieser appears in the Special Issue ahead of Clark and Rowlinson in arguing that there "have been various calls in the literature more recently for engaging with history in the study of organisations and their management" (pp. 321–321).[11] They go on to state that the call for more historical awareness in organization studies has "spurred some controversy" (p. 321), citing Kieser (1984) and "also Clark and Rowlinson's article in this issue" (p. 329.) The reference to Kieser is likely referring to the rejoiner by Paul Goldman, whereas the reference to the Clark and Rowlinson article is likely referring to an earlier reception to a previous (unpublished) version of the paper (see below).[12]

History in translation

Much of the Usdiken and Kieser (2004) article reproduces the claims from the earlier Kieser (1984) article but there is a more open and optimistic tone than the previous call, as seen in the opening comment about "various calls" for more history. What is also different is the introduction of a framework for judging different organizational approaches to history, which Usdiken and Kieser label "supplementarist, integrationist and reorientationist" (p. 322). For Usdiken and Kieser, the *supplementarist position* "views organisational studies as fundamentally social scientistic, and merely adds history as another contextual variable" (Bryman et al., 2011, p. 443). Arguably, this approach characterizes what Rowlinson (2004) refers to as the factual approach. The *integrationist position* "which seeks to enrich organization theory by developing links with the humanities, including history, literary theory and philosophy, without completely abandoning a social scientistic orientation" (Bryman et al., 2011, p. 443). This position is the one favoured by Usdiken and Kieser and they also link it to the work of Zald. Finally, the *reorientationist position* "involves moving organisation studies away from its social scientistic aspirations that are based on the natural sciences model. . . . In this broad reorienting sense, it is the social scientistic framing of organisation studies that is being challenged. With respect to the relation between history and organisation studies, it is not only the general a-historic character of the field that is being questioned but also the supplementarist and integrationist positions reviewed above that are rendered as 'problematic'" (Usdiken & Kieser,

2004, p. 324). Usdiken and Kieser go on to associate this approach with Rowlinson and his colleagues, specifically Carter, McKinlay and Rowlinson (2002). Later, Booth and Rowlinson (2006) went on to identify with this position.

What we can see here is something of a shift from the idea of a singular or unitary approach to history and its fit with a singular or unitary organization studies, to the idea of diverse approaches to history and to organization studies. It touches on the notion, raised by Zald (1989), that before history and organization studies can be integrated there needs to be an epistemological shift in both domains, but specifically organization studies – away from social scientistic to humanist forms of making sense of organizations. Through the outlining of three history positions to resolving some form of integration with organization studies, Usdiken and Kieser foreshadow, but do not develop, the ideas that there are likely different historical perspectives on organization studies.

The article by Leblebici and Shah (2004) is similar in tone and content of the discussion to that of Usdiken and Kieser (2004), even to the endorsement of the three categories of dealing with the role of history in organization studies. However, while Usdiken and Kieser focus on making a case for (more) historical perspectives in organization studies and some form of integration, Leblebici and Shah focus on finding a way to bring this about, arguing that we need to look for "an intersection of history and organisation theory where a fruitful dialogue can be established between these two domains of inquiry" (p. 356). They begin, like Usdiken and Kieser do, with the argument that there are growing calls for more historical accounts within organization studies. Indeed, they contend that "a large number of [organizational] scholars" . . . have "argued that we need to take history seriously" (p. 353). They then ask, "what does this mean" and "how are we to judge"?

History in translation

Leblebici and Shah suggest three possible answers to their question of how organizational scholars should take history seriously. The first is "to argue that our theories and empirical investigations only implicitly consider history." Here Leblebici and Shah contend that such indirect treatments of history "limits our understanding of organisational phenomena as well as the inclusion of history as an essential part of the field's development. The second answer, "and probably the most radical, is to argue that that neither our theories nor empirical investigations include any

history at all and that no social science can be without history."
The third answer, and the one most agreeable to Leblebici and
Shah, "is to argue that what is needed is to identify the terrain
where history and organisational studies meet. It is here that
both fields can make contributions to each others' efforts without dominating the other" (p. 353). Here they make three major
points. First, they contend that it is not interdisciplinarity that
will bring about some form of fusion between organization studies and history but rather "the choice of questions [asked] is the
most important factor in establishing such collaboration" (p. 353).
Thus, history needs to address "some of the most important questions discussed in organisational theory" while organisation theory needs to move away from the idea that history is not simply
a longer version of a case study" (p. 353). Second, they make a
detailed argument for convincing both historians and organizational scholars that "both theory and history are narratives uti-
lising similar tools," especially in the case of "process theories of
organisation where the sequences of events are the building blocks
of theory and history" (p. 356). Third, they focus on types of
agency-structural arrangements/interactions that shape organizational outcomes. These include "Iterational Elements" where the
agents involved are influence by the past to pay selective attention
to on-going activities; "Projective Elements" of a narrative which
"open up future possibilities and provide alternatives for the reso-
lution of conflicts" (p. 360), and "Practical-Evaluative Elements"
where agents are able to contextualize their social experience and
"are capable of creating open-ended and contingent sequences of
political action" (p. 360). The idea being that different interplays
of past experience and current structures influence the potential
for different forms of agency – an approach that can help to bridge
history and organization studies through focus on a particular set
of past experiences and current structures. Thus, "organisational
history must include the social structure, the cultural order, the
technology and the languages of the organisations that require the
investigator's careful interpretations" (p. 355).

While Leblebici and Shah offer some useful ideas for ways to focus
on the past that can attract both historians and organizational scholars they continue to conceptualize history and organization studies
from a disciplinary lens. History is largely spoken of in a unitary
vein, namely, that history is only what historians do. Similarly, organization studies is viewed as a particular discipline that is organized

around the study of the function and administration of organizations. As E.P. Thompson (1983, p. 15) once put it, sometimes it seems that "methodology is being used in the place of theory."

Clark and Rowlinson (2004): a review

Both Usdiken and Kieser (2004) and Leblebici and Shah (2004) preface the arguments of Clark and Rowlinson (2004) and Rowlinson (2004) that same year. Namely, that to affect a historic turn both history and organization studies need to be rethought in much the way it was being done in the discipline of History (a form of history that presumes the existence of a meta-narrative) (Ermarth, 1992; Jenkins, 1991; Scott, 1987; White, 1973) and among poststructuralist organizational scholars (Boje, Gephart, & Thatchenkery, 1996; Calás & Smircich, 1997; Cooper & Burrell, 1988).

There are three crucial aspects to Clark and Rowlinson article: (i) the appearance of a historic call, (ii) the lay out of the argument for a historic turn, and (iii) the context in which the call was made:

First, right from the opening sentence Clark and Rowlinson (2004, p. 331) appear to be commenting on a historic turn that is well underway. They state that there "is an increasing call for an historical perspective in organisation studies" (p. 331), which they then link to a supposed historic turn taking place across "other branches of the social sciences and humanities" (p. 331) – in the USA.[13] Nonetheless, they agree with McDonald (1996, p. 1) that history is a "contentious and by no means well-defined term."

Second, rather than talking about ways to fuse together some aspects of disciplinary history with organization studies, Clark and Rowlinson lay out some of the barriers to such a relationship. In particular, they proceed "to assess the major research programmes in organization studies in relation to the 'historic' turn" (p. 331) and to outline what a historic turn would look like. However, rather than defining organization studies, Clark and Rowlinson (2004, p. 332) "view organisation studies and related areas of strategy as a cluster of research programmes held together by the discourse of specific communities of theorists with overlapping interests" (p. 332). This clearly marks a shift from previous discussions of the (assumed) character of organization studies as a field of enquiry. From their perspective, a historic turn would (i) "represent a turn *against* the view that organisation studies should constitute a branch of the science of society" (p. 331, italics in original); (ii) involve "a contentious and by no means well-defined turn towards history – as past, process, context, and so on"; and (iii) "would entail a turn to historiographical debates and historical theories of interpretation that recognise the inherent ambiguity of the term 'history' itself, which refers to both 'the totality of past human actions, and . . . the narrative or account we construct of them" (p. 331).

Third, it is when Clark and Rowlinson (2002, p. 331) turn to the context in which a historical turn is occurring do we get further glimpse of how they are characterizing history:

> The historic turn is part of a wider transformation that is alluded to in terms such as the "discursive turn," deconstruction and post-modernism. Within history itself this transformation is associated with hermeneutics, the "linguistic turn," and the revival of narrative. *However, we feel that the term "historic turn" may prove useful in marshalling support for calls for more history, and a different approach to history, within organisation studies, rather than subsuming it under labels that do not emphasise the historical aspect.*
> (Clark & Rowlinson, 2004, p. 331, our emphasis)

They make the same point later in the paper, when they say that whether or not Burrell (1997) or Jacques (1996) "would associate themselves with a historic turn, each of them has identified particular problems in the prevailing approaches to history in organization studies which set the scene *for our review*"[14] (p. 332, our emphasis). Here Clark and Rowlinson seem to be arguing that the idea of a historic turn can be a useful heuristic for encouraging further interest in the use of history in organization studies but also a precursor to opening debate around the character of the study of history. The latter issue would loom larger in Booth and Rowlinson (2006) article. Before moving further into the debate, Clark and Rowlinson (2004) readily admit that "an argument can be made that organisation studies has already become more historical," and in this regard they cite new institutional economics, new institutionalism, path dependence theory, and the "rise of the organisational culture and symbolism discourse" (pp. 331–332). They go on to contend that as part of their review they "want to question whether, even as organisation studies has become more historical, the treatment of history could be said to correspond to an historic turn" (p. 332). This questioning forms the central focus of the paper. Thus, they undertake their review from "a sceptical standpoint" (p. 332).

History in translation
In 2015 Mick Rowlinson provided a retrospective "personal reflection" on what the historic turn means to [him]" (Rowlinson, 2015,

p. 70).[15] It represents an interesting account of how knowledge, specifically historical knowledge, is produced.

According to Rowlinson's (2015) account, an early version of the "historic turn" paper was submitted to the Management History Division of the *Academy of Management* (AoM) conference in Toronto, 2000. We have no information on how the original idea of the paper was first developed or even what the original idea was. We do learn from Rowlinson (2015), however, this was his first ever submission to the AoM and that the paper was rejected (Rowlinson, 2015, p. 72). Two of the three reviewers suggested that the paper be rejected, while the third reviewer classified the paper as "weak" but should nonetheless be accepted. In all three cases the reviewers made little comment, and what they had to say suggests lack of interest and/or a lack of expertise on the focus of the paper. One reviewer felt that the authors made their point well – namely, that "approaches/theories in organization studies" are generally ahistorical." However, he or she was concerned that the paper would not be of sufficient interest to members of the Management History Division; adding that the paper was "full of scholarly debate and short on evidence" (Rowlinson, 2015, p. 72). A second reviewer was tenuous about the value of the paper yet, paradoxically, definitive in his or her conclusion: "This is way outside my area of expertise, but my semi-educated guess is that it's not a very good paper & should probably be rejected" (Rowlinson, 2015, p. 72). The third reviewer critiqued the writing style, arguing that it could be "simplified and the paragraphs shortened for ease of reading" (Rowlinson, 2015, p. 72).

From this first set of clues we might speculate that Clark and Rowlinson's paper did not get accepted due to its novelty for the audience in question; a lack of fit with the main players in the MH Division at the time; a possible sufficient lack of networking by Clark and Rowlinson with some of the key decision makers in the Division at that time; little experience of engagement by Clark and Rowlinson with the intended audience. Also, the first mentioned reviewer suggests that the paper was not so much (if at all) about a historic turn as a critique of organization studies' failure to engage with history.

Having been rejected by the MH Division, Clark and Rowlinson went on to submit "a slightly modified version of the paper to a stream of the 2001 European Group for Organization Studies (EGOS) conference in Lyon (Rowlinson, 2015, p. 72). The paper was now titled: "The Treatment of History in Organization

Studies." The stream, *Re-discovering History in Studying Organizations*, was organized by Behlul Usdiken and Alfred Kieser. What we learn from the process is that the "slightly modified" paper did not refer to a historic turn; made no reference to McDonald's (1996) book; and was submitted to EGOS in the hope that the stream "might be more receptive" to the authors' ideas than the Management History Division of the AoM (Rowlinson, 2015, p. 72). The paper was accepted and subsequently presented. Rowlinson can't remember how the paper was received but speculates that "it must have gone reasonably well to [subsequently be] selected for the special issue of *Business History*" (Rowlinson, 2015, p. 73). What we will note here is that the structures and process of AoM and EGOS differ in important ways that may have affected the acceptance of the early paper and/or the slightly modified paper. Generally, EGOS streams are one-off events that bring together a number of scholars who, broadly speaking, share an interest in research topics related to the theme of the steam. For example, to run a stream a group of scholars need to submit a proposal to the EGOS organizers. Usually streams are organized around specific themes, such as "History and New Institution Theory," that will be limited to those scholars with a *particular interest* in history and new institution theory. Those running a stream have the authority to find their own reviewers and to decide which papers to accept and which ones to reject. They are only limited by the number of papers they are allowed to accept and those are usually around a maximum of 30 papers. In contrast, the Management History Division of the AoM is a standing body of scholars, many of whom regularly attend the division.[16] This arguably provides opportunities for structural power in the form of election to the division's leadership,[17] and discursive power in the form of influences on determining what type of research (i.e., favoured ontologies, epistemologies, methodologies, theoretic perspectives, etc.) is acceptable for presentation and what type is not so privileged.[18] The Program Chair is elected from the membership of the division and plays a discretionary role in accepting and rejecting papers and symposia that are allocated for reviews based on the algorithm referring to fifty key words.[19] Thus, we might speculate that the different processes involved may have affected the acceptance status of each version of the Clark and Rowlinson paper. In the case of the 2000 MH Division Clark and Rowlinson were likely vying for acceptance in a field of papers that were largely empirical and possibly atheoretical. Whereas the 2001 EGOS stream was organized around a group of papers that broadly focused on the same areas of concern viz. the relationship between history and organization studies.

In September 2001, two months following the EGOS conference, Usdiken and Kieser contacted Clark and Rowlinson to tell that that their paper had been "selected . . . for inclusion in a proposal for a special issue of *Business History* that they would soon be submitting to the journal. They went on to ask for an "abstract for a *revised version* of the paper" (Rowlinson, 2015, p. 73, our emphasis). The abstract, which was sent the following day, mentioned, "for the first time," the historic turn (Ibid.). In fact, the historic turn was stated "in much bolder terms" than hitherto (Ibid.). The abstract read: In this paper we call for a "historic turn in organization studies along the lines of the turn towards history that has transformed other fields in the social sciences and humanities" (Ibid.).

Somehow or other the idea of a historic turn was retained from this point on but in a more toned down, tenuous manner. Over the next three months there was, according to Rowlinson (2015, p. 73), something of a dialogue between Peter Clark and Alfred Kieser on the further development and revision of the paper. Kieser advised Clark to remove specific sections of the paper that did not seem relevant and/or were difficult to understand (Ibid.).[20] Clark accepted this advice. Later, following publication of the article, Clark and Rowlinson thanked "Alfred Kieser and Behlul Usdiken, for organizing the [EGOS] sub-theme . . . and for their help in developing this article" (Clark & Rowlinson, 2004, p. 347). But the article wasn't there yet. Clark and Rowlinson had to go through a new round of reviews.

The two EGOS reviews proved to be fateful. In sharing the reviews with Clark and Rowlinson, Alfred Kieser commented that he was attaching the reviewers' comments, so that they [Clark and Rowlinson] could "read them for [themselves] so that he [didn't] have to reiterate them in detail" (email from Alfred Kieser to Peter Clark and Mick Rowlinson, July 14, 2002, quoted in Rowlinson, 2015, p. 74). Kieser went on to state that he "very much hope[d]" that the authors would decide to rewrite the paper (Rowlinson, 2015, p. 74). This suggested to Clark and Rowlinson that this "was a formidable invitation to revise and resubmit" the paper (Rowlinson, 2015, p. 74). The reviews seem to bear that out. Reviewer 1 asked the authors "to strip away the platitudes, the academic posturing, the glossy jargon and get down to basics? He or she also expressed the view that the paper was overly theoretical and the authors "have no credibility with practitioners" (Rowlinson, 2015, p. 74). Reviewer 2, meantime seemed to be unhappy with the authors' argument that "most business historians [are] common sense empiricists," adding, rather curiously, that "the explicit policy of [*Business History*] is to publish theory-informed articles (even if not all of those published would fulfill the requirement)" (Rowlinson, 2015, p. 75).[21] In the subsequent engagement with the reviewers, in the form of a revised paper and a written response, the paper's title changed somewhat. In response to Reviewer 2 Clark and Rowlinson added, for clarification, the subtitle "Toward an Historic Turn?" – "albeit, with an ironic question mark" (Rowlinson, 2015, p. 75). There were no further reviews and the paper was published in the special issue in July 2004.

Later, reflecting on the overall process, Rowlinson (2015, p. 75) went on to wonder "how significant it was that the historic turn acquired the name at that particular time."[22] He goes on to point out that, nonetheless, the paper has been fairly widely disseminated, with the second highest citation count of any previous articles in *Business History* and with the special issue itself being the sixth most cited in that journal.

By way of a conclusion, Rowlinson (2015, p. 78) argues that if the idea of a historic turn "provides a convenient label for an emerging network of scholars then it has more than served its purpose. Now that this network is becoming more established it seems appropriate for us to create our own etiological myths, and it would be gratifying if our articles continue to be seen as the origin of the historic turn to describe a more self-consciously historical orientation within organization studies."

From our own reflections we observe the following. First, the role of Alfred Kieser was not inconsequential in either getting an EGOS stream accepted by the EGOS conference organizers, or in getting a proposal for a special issue accepted by the editorial group of *Business History*. He would also have played a key role in deciding which papers to accept for the EGOS stream and which papers to follow up for inclusion in the special issue. He is a "key figure"[23] in the development of E.G.O.S., becoming Chair in 2000.[24] He is also a founding editor of *Organization Studies* and, as stated above, it was at the 1993 Colloquium of EGOS where he was invited to present his paper on "Why Organization Theory needs Historical Analysis." Roland Calori, the overall EGOS conference organizer, was also associated with the history steam at the 2001 EGOS Colloquium. According to Usdiken and Kieser (2004, p. 328), Calori was "very enthusiastic throughout" and was also one of the reviewers involved in the special issue.[25]

Our second observation – based on Rowlinson's own assessment – was that both EGOS reviewers were relatively critical, especially Reviewer 1, who Rowlinson (2015, pp. 74–75) "strongly suspect[ed] was in favour of rejecting" the article. Given the eminence of the scholars involved in the review process we suggest that Usdiken and Kieser had to make a decision that was not in line with at least one reviewer of some stature in the field of business history and/or organization studies.[26]

Our third observation is that part of the reason how and why the idea of the historic turn became fairly widely disseminated was the existence of an "emerging network" (Rowlinson, 2015), or "sub-community" (Kieser, 2015) of scholars that, arguably, formed the basis of a "historically oriented" paradigm within management and organizational studies. However, as we shall see in the next chapter, the "sub-community" – if in fact it is constituted as a community – is more or less held together by not questioning the very idea of being "historically oriented." This vague focus may well have helped to this point to encourage a popular front of assorted "historically oriented" scholars and thus assisted the process of dissemination. However, as Rowlinson (2004), himself, was to contend, the emerging field (of Management and Organizational History?) includes at least three main perspectives – factual, narrative, and archaeo-genealogical[27] – with profoundly different ontological, epistemological and methodological stances (see Chapter 1 above).[28] This very much has the making of the development of a paradigm, with all the trappings of emerging differences and exclusions (Kuhn, 1962).[29] At least in the short turn a heated and protracted debate might contribute to further dissemination of the historic turn. An example is the work of Bradley Bowden, the editor of the *Journal of Management History*, whose book – *Work, Wealth & Postmodernism. The intellectual conflict at the heart of business endeavour* (2018) – centers his attack on Clark and Rowlinson's (2004) article and specifically the historic turn. He contends that the article is problematic for its "pure Foucauldian" view of "'history' [as] not something that is objectively real but is instead 'the narrative or account we construct'" (Bowden, 2018, p. 212). Bowden goes on to opine that: "The unwillingness of advocates of the Historic Turn (Mills and Durepos excepted) to carefully explain the theoretical roots of their intellectual positions exposes them to significant, if as yet unacknowledged, conceptual, and methodological problems; problems that undermine the credibility of their critiques of modernity" (Bowden, 2018, pp. 215–216). Nonetheless, he also states that "Meanwhile, support for the historic turn [has] attracted an ever-increasing following" (p. 213).

Our fourth observation is that the argument for a historic turn underwent different foci and meanings before becoming more or less fixed or "blackboxed" (Latour, 2005) as a call for more historically oriented studies of management and organization studies. As we have seen above, the idea seemed to come into play as a clear argument[30] for the inclusion of "historical analyses in organization theory" (Kieser, 1994), moving away from Zald's critique of the scientistic character of organization. Then, in the hands of Clark and Rowlinson, the focus returned to a kind of Zaldian critique of "the treatment of history in organization studies" (Clark and Rowlinson, rejected 2000 Academy of Management paper; accepted 2001 EGOS paper; first submission to 2004 *Business History* special issue; Rowlinson, 2004). Then, briefly, it became a strong call for a historic turn in MOS (Clark and Rowlinson initial abstract submitted to the Usdiken and Kieser proposal for a special issue; numerous post-2004 citations supporting the idea of a historic turn). The next iteration was in three ways a more tenuous argument for a historic turn. The argument itself was more tenuous, signaled through the added subtitle and the ending question-mark. But there was also the inclusion of the historic turn as a heuristic, a way of encouraging more debate around the relationship between history and MOS. Yet, the argument for a historic turn is also simultaneously strengthened through reference to McDonald (1996) and his claims of a historic turn in the social sciences and humanities.

This then lends itself to some oscillation between the two ideas of turn versus heuristic (Clark and Rowlinson, 2004; Rowlinson, 2015). Currently, despite debate around the need for a historic turn (A. J. Mills et al., 2016) and what it means, the idea itself is produced and reproduced as an established thing.

In 2006 the initial "historic turn" took yet another turn in Booth and Rowlinson's (2006) "10-point agenda, with proposals for future directions in management and organizational history" (p. 5). As we shall see in the next chapter, the idea of the historic turn takes a new, more concrete, tack that will lead to a new generation of citations that reference

Booth and Rowlinson (2006) as the foundational article. In the following "10-point agenda" they laid out key ideas for "future directions in management and organizational history" (p. 5). As we shall see below, although the stated intent of the article (and the launch of *Management & Organizational History*) was "to stimulate debate, not to define boundaries or exclude other possibilities" (Booth & Rowlinson, 2006, p. 5) debate is largely viewed through an archaeo-genealogical lens: a lens that is meant to serve as a unifying force.

Notes

1 The Special Issue included articles by both authors of this book – with Mills writing on Maslow and Gender and Novicevic writing on Barnard and leadership!

2 As part of, what was to become, the lead up to the launch of *M&OH*, a well-attended symposium on "Management and Organizational History – The Future of the Past" was held at the Academy of Management annual conference, in New Orleans, in August 2004. Among the panelist was Mick Rowlinson, Bill Cooke, Stephen Proctor, Ann Rippin, Jean Helms Mills, Lois Kurowski, Emma Bell, Albert J. Mills, John Wilson, John Hassard, and Richard Marens. All of these participants were to become members of the *M&OH* editorial board, with Kurowski and Marens as Assistant Editors. Mayer Zald was also a member of the editorial board. Discerning readers will spot the connections across some of the people and events we have chosen to highlight!

3 While Zald, Kieser, Jacques, and Burrell are cited as exemplars in Clark and Rowlinson (2004), Jacques does not appear in Booth and Rowlinson (2006) but Stewart Clegg's name has been added to the list. With that in mind, and as we are focusing on Clark and Rowlinson's (2004) exemplar, we have not included Steward Clegg at this stage.

4 The outlining of each of the four points is quoted directly from Bryman, Bell, Mills, and Yue (2011, pp. 433–435).

5 We should note here that Rowlinson's (2004) expressed intent was not to pass value judgements on different "variants" of historical perspectives. Rather, he argued that to understand the call for a historic turn we need to assess what this means (what is being called for) across different perspectives. That is pretty much what we are doing here in this chapter.

6 To be perfectly clear, while we are distancing ourselves from this kind of approach we are not claiming to have been above the fray and thus we are not pointing fingers here but are responsible for similar styles of writing elsewhere.

7 Kieser has since gone on to question the socio-political and cultural locations in which the study of organizations and history are conceptualized (see Kieser, 1997, 2004).

8 This includes the works of Kanter (1977), Wolff (1977), Benson (1978), Hearn and Parkin (1983), Burrell (1984), Gutek (1985), Mills and Tancred (1992), Calás (1992), Calás and Smircich (1992), Bell and Nkomo (1992), and many more. Much of this work also analysed the extent to

which gender was largely absent from organization studies and theorizations. It was also a time frame when feminist historians and philosophers were influencing discussions on work and organization, including Sheila Rowbotham (1999), Joan Wallach Scott (1987), Annette Kuhn and Annmarie Wolpe (1978), Gayatri Chakravorty Spivak (1987), Natalie Zemon Davis (1983), Elizabeth Ermarth (1992), Elizabeth Fox-Genovese (1982), and many others.

9 See also Burrell (1987). Interestingly enough Rowlinson (2004) does not draw on Burrell's *Pandemonium* but rather two other of this works as exemplars of the historic turn, namely Burrell (1988) and (1998).

10 While there were several articles in this Special Issue we selected, in addition to the article by Clark and Rowlinson, only those that directly engaged in debate around issues of the integration of history and organization studies.

11 Here they cite Zald (1989) and Kieser (1994).

12 The Special Issue was "based on a selection from the papers presented at the sub-theme entitled 'Re-discovering History in Studying Organisations' that [was] convened at the 17th EGOS (European Group for Organizational Studies) Colloquium held in Lyon, France, 3–5 July 2001" (Usdiken & Kieser, 2004, p. 328).

13 Here they cite T. J. McDonald (1996), and it may be useful to surface some aspects of this article at this stage. First thing of note is that McDonald refers to history in quotes – i.e., "history." He goes on to argue that the transformation of the humanities and social sciences "*in America today*" (p. 1, our emphasis) is "'historic' in at least three senses. First, it represents an epochal turn *against* the science of society constituted at least in part in opposition to 'history' in the immediate post-World War. Second, it involves a contentious and by no means well-defined turn *toward* history. . . . Finally, it is producing renewed inquiry into the construction *in* history of disciplinary discourses and investigators" (p. 1, emphasis in the original). McDonald also notes that the concern with a historic turn is not new – citing C. Wright Mills' (1959, p. 145) call for "every social science – or better, every well-considered social study – requires an historical scope of conception and a full use of historical materials" (cited in McDonald, 1996, p. 3). McDonald (1996, p. 3) contends that

> historical work had by no means stopped in the 1950s and 1960s, [but] voices like Mills stood out because of a variety of seemingly disparate developments in *the United States* that seemed to add up to a declaration of the 'end' of history.

(Our emphasis)

14 To be clear, Clark and Rowlinson address the same concern to all four exemplary scholars but, from our reading, they suggest that Zald and Kieser take a more obvious, or direct, stance on the relationship between history and organization studies.

15 To give him his due, this was a very courageous move given that it revealed much of the critique of his work that preceded publication. It also reveals something of the process and the numerous actors that go into the production of knowledge.

16 Founded in 1971, the Management History Division was one of the first to be established, alongside eight other divisions. Among the other eight were the Organization Management Theory Division and the Organizational Behavior Division.

17 Both authors have served on the Divisional leadership. Milorad was the Division Chair in 2014, and Albert served as the Member at Large from 2016 to 2019.

18 For an account of the influence of AoM leaders at national and divisional level see Grant and Mills (2006) and Myrick, Helms Mills and Mills (2013).

19 Program Chairs usually serve for a period of five years as a member of the division's executive committee rotating in the roles of the PDW chair, the Division Chair, and the Past Chair.

20 The deleted sections included ones referring to "Burrell, Bauman and the Holocaust and bureaucracy," and one on "Analytically Structured Narrative."

21 As the review process was blinded, we cannot know who the specific reviewers were but Usdiken and Kieser (2004, p. 328) provide some important clues as to who they might have been. In a note at the end of their article, Usdiken and Kieser (2004, p. 328) thanked those "colleagues who helped as reviewers in the preparation of this special issue," including

> Rolv Petter Amdam (Norwegian School of Management, Norway), Finn Borum (Copenhagen Business School, Denmark), Haldor Byrkjeflot (Stein Rokkan Center of Social Studies, Norway), the late Roland Calori (EM Lyon, France), Paula Carson (University of Louisiana, USA), Mark Casson (University of Reading, UK), Bob Hinings (University of Alberta, Canada), Paul Hirsch (Northwestern University, USA), Matthias Kipping (Universitat Pompeu Fabra, Spain), Jean-Claude Thoenig (GAPP-CNRS, France), Richard Whittington (University of Oxford, UK), Daniel Wren (University of Oklahoma, USA).

22 From an anti-postmodernist perceptive, Bradley Bowden (2018, p. 212) answers: "There is little doubt that Clark and Rowlinson's article would not have had the impact that it did had it been published 10 or even 5 years earlier" (p. 212). He seems to base this assessment on the claim that by 2004 postmodernism was a spent force in Management and Organization Studies and Management and Organizational History.

23 www.egosnet.org/jart/prj3/egos/main.jart?rel=de&content-id=1334581193767&reserve-mode=reserve.

24 That was the year before the history stream at which Clark and Rowlinson presented an earlier version of their paper.

25 Sadly, Calori's suffered an untimely and unexpected death during the process and Usdiken and Kieser devoted the Special Issue to him.

26 As the review process was blinded, we cannot know who the specific reviewers were on the Clark and Rowlinson paper, but Usdiken and Kieser (2004, p. 328) provide some important clues as to who they might have been. In a note at the end of their article, Usdiken and Kieser (2004, p. 328) thanked those "colleagues who helped as reviewers in the preparation of this special issue," including

Rolv Petter Amdam (Norwegian School of Management, Norway), Finn Borum (Copenhagen Business School, Denmark), Haldor Byrkjeflot (Stein Rokkan Center of Social Studies, Norway), the late Roland Calori (EM Lyon, France), Paula Carson (University of Louisiana, USA), Mark Casson (University of Reading, UK), Bob Hinings (University of Alberta, Canada), Paul Hirsch (Northwestern University, USA), Matthias Kipping (Universitat Pompeu Fabra, Spain), Jean-Claude Thoenig (GAPP-CNRS, France), Richard Whittington (University of Oxford, UK), Daniel Wren (University of Oklahoma, USA).

27 We would add a fourth perspective – amodernist (Durepos, 2015; Durepos & Mills, 2018).

28 These differences underline the fragility of the existing community, a fragility that is clear to see in Bradley Bowden's (2018) onslaught on postmodern (and, to a somewhat lesser degree, amodernist) approaches to history. Unfortunately, at least for Durepos and Mills, Bowden (2018) confuses postmodernism with amodernism: "Readers of Gabrielle Durepos and Albert Mills' *ANTi-History* are left in no doubt as to their postmodernist – or to be exact, *amodernist* – allegiances, with the authors declaring that ANTi-History draws on Foucault's scholarship" (p. 215). The difference between the two will be dealt with in Chapter 4.

29 At the center of Bowden's attack on postmodernist history is Clark and Rowlinson's (2004) article, which he contends is problematic for its "pure Foucauldian" view of "'history' [as] not something that is objectively real but is instead 'the narrative or account we construct'" (p. 212). Bowden goes on to opine that:

> The unwillingness of advocates of the Historic Turn (Mills and Durepos excepted) to carefully explain the theoretical roots of their intellectual positions exposes them to significant, if as yet unacknowledged, conceptual, and methodological problems; problems that undermine the credibility of their critiques of modernity.
>
> (pp. 215–216)

30 We have chosen this paper as an illustrative example because it is centrally an argument about the relationship between history and organization theory. It could arguably be read as a call for a historic turn, albeit without specific naming it as such. In fact, Rowlinson (2015, p. 71) provides a useful contrast when discussing the historical approach of Jacques (1996), Burrell (1997), and Clegg (1989): they tend "to overlook relevant historiographical debates . . . and rely on particular historiographical interpretations that appealed to their own historical sensibilities."

4 Paradigms and prospects in management and organizational history

In 2006 Charles Booth and Mick Rowlinson launched the journal *Management & Organizational History*, with an editorial that set out a ten-point agenda for the development of a distinct field of "organizational history" (Booth & Rowlinson, 2006, p. 12). In the process, the new *Management & Organizational History* journal would serve as a research venue for the emerging field of organizational history. To make their case for this new sub-field,[1] Booth and Rowlinson provide historical context for its emergence, starting with the 'historic turn' that is arguably taking place in management and organization theory"[2] (p. 5). They then contend that debates around the need for a historic turn have encouraged "increasing reflection on appropriate styles of writing about organizations historically"[3] and "increasing attention to philosophers of history in organization studies"[4] (Booth & Rowlinson, 2006, p. 12). The remaining six agenda items constitute a far-ranging critique and engagement with functionalist sociological accounts of organizational culture and collective memory"[5] and of the focus and method of business history and theory,[6] business ethics in history,[7] metanarratives of corporate capitalism,[8] management history and management education,[9] and the dangers of public history to further narrow the idea of history (i.e., as a factualist approach to understanding the past).[10]

Debates within MOH

Through their review of contextual factors that led to a new sub-field, Booth and Rowlinson (2006) provide some clues to debates within the emergent field.

The historic turn

The call for "a more historical approach to management and organizations" (Booth & Rowlinson, 2006, p. 6) continues unabated.[11] While they refer back to issues of universalism and presentism as reasons for organization studies to take a more historic approach, Booth and Rowlinson (2006, p. 7) also attempt to broaden the debate by contending that calls "for more historic awareness are often aligned with critical management studies" (CMS).[12] They go on to state that "the historic turn also involves more critical and ethical reflection" (Booth & Rowlinson, 2006, p. 7) – citing work on race, gender, sexuality, and postcolonial theory.[13] This moves us from an earlier focus on a paradigmatically undifferentiated to a paradigmatically differentiated notion of history (Rowlinson, 2004). In the process it privileges CMS[14] and Foucauldian approaches to history and the past. From this perspective it can be argued that the historic turn had been largely resolved within certain communities of practice long before the earlier "calls" for a historic turn. This is at its clearest among adherents of postmodernism[15] where, for example, the notion of discourse is applied to extant and past knowledge. Here we have forms of analysis applied across different epistemes. Thus, arguably, adherents of Foucauldian analysis were not simply calling for a historic turn *within* organization studies but a radical change in the way such studies are conceived and take account of history and the role of the past (Burrell, 1988; Jacques, 1996; Munslow, 2015). However, this is not to say that all postmodernist organizational theorists (a) agree on the idea of history, or that (b) they are all concerned with history.[16]

Historical methods and styles of writing

In their second agenda point, Booth and Rowlinson (2006, p. 8) contend that the historic turn "raises questions about methods and appropriate styles of writing for more historically oriented research." We would argue that it is not simply the historic turn that has raised questions about methods and writing styles but critiques of scientistic and objectivist methods[17] but especially the search for new and critical paradigms for the study of history in organization studies. As examples of alternative ways of studying the past Booth and Rowlinson (2006) offer two main examples. The first is attention to the work of Burrell (1997) who, they note "eschews the aura of realism and objectivity . . . avoiding anything resembling a conventional chronological narrative" (p. 9). The second is the work of Whipp and Clark (1986), who proposed "analytically structured narratives" (Booth and Rowlinson, 2006, p. 9). It is an approach situated

> on the bridge between narrative and analytical schemas . . . in an attempt to strike a balance between atheoretical common-sense, empirical historical accounts of what really happened, and

overtheorized, sociological or economic accounts which explain the structural or economic necessity underlying events that have already been recounted by historians.

(p. 9)

It is a methodological approach that Booth and Rowlinson (2006) seem to have some sympathy with but don't make much more of it.[18]

Philosophers of history and historical theorists

This third agenda point seems to serve three purposes:

1   To encourage "further engagement with the philosophy of history and historical theorist" (p. 10); this is possibly linked to debates within the discipline of history itself that were influencing management theorists and historians who were turning away from factualist accounts and seeking alternative ways of conceptualizing organization studies (Burrell & Morgan, 1979; Clegg, 1981; Clegg & Dunkerley, 1977, 1980);

2   To suggest leading historical theorists that might be relevant to management and organizational studies (MOS) with Hayden White (1973, 1987), Michel Foucault (1970, 1972), Paul Ricoeur (1984), David Carr (1986), and Deirdre McCloskey (1994)[19]; surprisingly, given their earlier references to feminism, postcolonialism, and ethics, there is no reference to postcolonial (e.g., Said, 1979, 1993) or feminist theorists of history (e.g., Scott, 1986, 1987)[20]; and

3   To raise issues about the role of narratives in management history. In this regard they point out Carr's notion of "narrative as the essence of human existence and consciousness in time" [which] differs from White and Foucault's impositionalist view that "narrative is an imposition on the part of the historian as narrator" (Booth & Rowlinson, 2006, p. 10). Here Booth and Rowlinson (2006, p. 10) seem to lean towards McCloskey's argument "that history 'is a story we tell', and that continuity and discontinuity are narrative devices, to be chosen for their storytelling virtues."

From corporate culture to public history

The remaining six agenda items form the base of a wide-ranging critique that largely engages with business history and functionalist theories of organization. Here Booth and Rowlinson (2006) view organizational culture as a potentially useful concept for tracing historical contexts (see Mills, 2006) but argue that it has been conflated with history as it has been increasingly popularized in the practitioner literature. As such, it can be argued, it has led to an "invented tradition" that "bears little relation to 'documented history'" (Booth & Rowlinson, 2006, p. 11).

Likewise, the notion of organizational memory, and its use value to organizational studies, has been characterized by positivist organizational theorists "as a store for objectified truth" (Ibid.). Booth and Rowlinson (2006, p. 12), on the other hand, see a connection to be explored "between social memory and organizational symbolism, arguing that the symbolic life of an organization includes the symbolism of the past and the practices whereby the past is remembered."

They further engage with business historians and their benign view of big business, critiquing the "consensus narrative" of Alfred Chandler and citing the work of Galambos "as looking beyond the firm to its political context, power relations, and links to the professions" while building on the work of Chandler (Booth & Rowlinson, 2006, p. 14).[21]

History in translation

Meantime, in the midst of these debates Wanderley and Faria (2012) offer up a different response to the focus and popularity of Chandler. They introduce a de-colonial account of the fate of two comparable and contemporary strategic management scholars – Alfred Chandler (USA) and Celso Furtado (Brazil). They show how Chandler's work became globally known and accepted, while Furtado's work was largely ignored outside of Brazil. They conclude that:

> For more than 50 years Chandler and Furtado approached corporations and the government from different perspectives. Only Chandler's contributions became recognised in the field of strategic management whereas Furtado's propositions were buried by the epistemic coloniality (Mignolo, 2007) of knowledge from the North.
>
> (Wanderley & Faria, 2012, p. 233)

Booth and Rowlinson (2006) move through critiques of business ethics (as an ahistorical sub-field of MOS), and the metanarratives of corporate capitalism that are imposed on studies of organization and mask the origins of management theory in a diverse range of debates. For example, in a later publication, Rowlinson goes on to claim that the notion of scientific management has its roots in President Teddy Roosevelt's concerns with conservation and his attempt to associate this with the idea of scientific management professionals (Cummings et al., 2017).

Finally, Booth and Rowlinson (2006) go on to warn of the dangers of management history (by which they seem to mean factualist accounts) that serve to reinforce the various associations of capitalism with the values of management studies, rather than encouraging students to question management theory as the outcome of power and the socio-politics of knowledge production. In a similar vein, Booth and Rowlinson (2006) suggest that the increasing popularization of public history may be in danger of reinforcing the idea that history provides factual accounts of actual or real events in time. Here they see a glimmer of hope in the development of counter histories whereby the author takes a known historical event (e.g., the defeat of Hitler) and asks "what if" the opposite had happened (e.g., that Hitler had won the Second World War)? Booth and Rowlinson contend that such histories have been a reaction of conservative and liberal "challenge[s] to the historical determinism that Marxists allegedly adhere to" (p. 21). Nonetheless, they continue, this "could also temper the determinism that prevails in the predominant theories of organization, and counterfactuals might be one way to counter such determinism."[22]

History in translation

Shortly before the founding of *Management & Organization History* (MOH) in 2006 Mick Rowlinson and colleagues invited a number of management and organizational historians to a "Symposium on Counterfactual History in Management and Organizations" at Warwick University in the UK, in December 2005. Many of the presentations subsequently found their way into the pages of the new MOH – see volumes 2 (issue 4), and 3 (issue 1) over 2007–2008. Two of the articles in Volume 3 (1) by Mads Mordhorst, and Gabrielle Durepos, Albert Mills and Jean Helms Mills were, respectively, earlier iterations of what has been called the Copenhagen School and the Halifax School (Bettin, Mills, & Helms Mills, 2016; Corrigan, 2015; Mills, Suddaby, Foster, & Durepos, 2016).

Notes

1 This is agenda item 5.
2 Agenda item 1.
3 Agenda item 2.
4 Agenda item 3.
5 Agenda item 4.

6 Agenda item 6.
7 Agenda item 7.
8 Agenda item 8.
9 Agenda item 9.
10 Agenda item 10.
11 More recently, Greenwood and Bernardi (2014, p. 912) "feel that is it is significant that, a quarter of a century after initial calls for the historical reorientation of OS, debates still continue to fill the journals and conference halls pondering why historical approaches are not more routinely incorporated into OS."
12 Here Booth and Rowlinson cite the work of Zald (2002), Burrell (1997) and Jacques (1996).
13 They cite, respectively, Nkomo (1992), Aaltio, Mills and Helms Mills (2002), Mills (2002, 2006), Thomas, Mills and Helms Mills (2004), Mills (1997), and Anshuman Prasad (1997). In the latter case, the quote Prasad as seeking "to theorize workplace diversity within the wider context of the (continuing?) history and experience of Euro-American imperialism and colonialism" (Booth & Rowlinson, 2006, p. 8).
14 CMS emerged as an Interest Group of the Academy of Management (AoM) in 1999, before becoming a Division in 2005. Concurrently, a bi-annual International Critical Management Studies conference was established in 1999. The current "domain name" of the CMS Division of the AoM reads as follows:

> CMS serves as a forum within the Academy for the expression of views critical of established management practices and the established social order. Our premise is that structural features of contemporary society, such as the profit imperative, patriarchy, racial inequality, and ecological irresponsibility often turn organizations into instruments of domination and exploitation. Driven by a shared desire to change this situation, we aim in our research, teaching, and practice to develop critical interpretations of management and society and to generate radical alternatives. Our critique seeks to connect the practical shortcomings in management and individual managers to the demands of a socially divisive and ecologically destructive system within which managers work.
>
> (http://aom.org/Divisions-and-Interest-Groups/Academy-of-Management-Division—Interest-Group-Domain-Statements.
> aspx#cms)

15 See endnote 5 above.
16 A study of the use of history across CMS communities (e.g., postcolonialist theorists, feminists, Marxists, and postmodernists) suggests that history is still undertheorized (Mills & Helms Mills, 2013). By way of example, the study revealed three major historical accounts of the development of CMS (Adler, Forbes, & Willmott, 2006; Burrell, Reed, Calás, Smircich, & Alvesson, 1994; Hassard, Hogan, & Rowlinson, 2001) that all differed in profound ways (Mills & Helms Mills, 2013).
17 Booth and Rowlinson (2006, p. 9) contend that "Historians, and especially business historians, are not expected to produce a methodological justification of their work." They give the example of archival works, arguing

that business historians' "copious notes detailing the locations of sources in the archive are usually seen as sufficient methodological justification in their own right" (p. 9). Elsewhere the relationship between paradigmatic grounding and archival research has been discussed at length (Burton, 2005a; Cifor & Wood, 2017; Decker, 2013; Schwarzkopf, 2012 – see also Chaper 1).

They go on to label business historians as "inveterate empiricists" (p. 13), who need to "engage with the epistemological questions concerning sources and historical narratives raised by organization theorists" (p.8). Interestingly, this critique is similar in characterization to the one objected to by the AoM's Reviewer 2 of the 2000 rejected Clark and Rowlinson paper (viz. the claim that "most business historians [are] common sense empiricists").

18 It may be recalled from Chapter 2, that a section on "analytically structured narratives" appeared in Clark and Rowlinson's submission to the 2006 Special Issue of *Business History* but was removed on the advice of Alfred Kieser who felt that is did not seem relevant and was difficult to understand.

19 The development of CMS reflected and contributed to the search for new theories of organization, with some turning to Marxism (Clegg, 1981), critical theory (Alvesson & Willmott, 1992), postmodernism (Burrell, 1998) – theories that also informed studies of the past and its influence on organization studies.

20 While McCloskey identifies as a feminist and she has done some work with the LGBT community her inclusion in the list of suggested philosophers is focused on her methodological work related to the value of capitalism.

21 Rowlinson has pursued the role of alternative starting points to this day to reveal their impact on how this changes our perception of historical accounts (Cummings, Bridgman, Hassard, & Rowlinson, 2017).

22 Arguably, counterfactuals have also been used, especially in literature, by left-wing writers to challenge the failure of conservative and reactionary historical accounts – see, for example, Philip Roth's "Plot Against America," New York, Random House, 2004; and Robert Harris' "Fatherland," Harmondsworth: Penguin, 2017.

5 Revisiting the historic turn ten years on[1]

With the approach of 2016 it appeared to some that it was time to take stock of the influence of "the idea of the historic turn (HT). To that end, Albert Mills, Roy Suddaby, Bill Foster, and Gabie Durepos approached Peter Miskell, the Editor of *Management & Organization History* (M&OH), and proposed a Special Issue of the journal around the theme of revisiting the HT. Peter agreed, and the Special Issue was published as Volume 11, number 2, May 2016. The issue consisted on eight papers and an introduction by Mills et al. The introduction began with a conclusion that the "historic turn" was "perhaps mislabeled and very much depends on what is seen as history and what is seen as constituting MOS" (Mills et al., 2016, p. 67). They went on to opine that there "are at least three alternative characterizations; first, a historic *re*turn to MOS; second, *rethinking* MOS from a historiographic perspective; and, third, critically interpreting MOS and its relationship to history and the past" (Ibid.).

The historic return

Here, Mills et al. (2016) made three main points. First, to concede the point that from the start of the 1980s, at least in the important area of U.S. management textbooks, there has been a considerable lessoning of the focus on history. Second, notwithstanding, a small but important number of management history scholars, mainly associated with the Management History Division of the Academy of Management, had managed to establish and develop noted histories of management theory, for example, Wren, Bedeian, and George (Novicevic, Jones, & Carraher, 2015). Third, we also note that the debate seems to have focused on changes within managerialist theory and history but needs to take into account discussions within other paradigmatic communities (e.g., feminism, Marxism, postcolonialism, postmodernism, and new institution theory) who continue to engage with/embrace history.[2]

Rethinking MOS from a historiographic perspective

This perspective refers to the early calls by Zald, Keiser, Booth, Clark, Rowlinson, etc. that aimed to "reintegrate historical analyses into organization theory" (Mills et al., 2016, p. 68). Yet it shares the same fatal flaw as the *generalized* call for a historical turn by treating MOS as a more-or-less unified field. Again, that does not take into account the constitution of various paradigmatic communities, whose history-making has to be understood in context!

Critically interrogating MOS and its relationship to history and the past

The third alternative refers to the space opened by Booth and Rowlinson (2006) and the founding of the *M&OH* journal. This led to further encouragement of critical interrogation of the relationship not only between management and organization studies (MOS) and history but also between history and the past. It is argued that in practice this process has taken us two steps forward and one step back. It is forward thinking because it has opened space for greater debate by (i) questioning the positivist grounding of much of MOS, (ii) encouraging new methods and ways of writing history, (iii) further engaging with philosophies of history, and (iv) seeking greater alignment between historical awareness and critical management studies. However, it has also taken one step backwards by seeming to privilege history over MOS, while, paradoxically, failing to problematize history.

History in translation

Analysis of the various articles in the "Re-visiting the Historic Turn" special issue provides further clues to the development of the sub-field of management and organizational history.

Given that the special issue was focused on *re-visiting* the historic turn we might expect that most if not all of the articles would have mentioned the historic turn. In fact, two of the eight articles (Brunninge & Melander, 2016; Zundel, Holt, & Popp, 2016) do not make any reference to the historical turn, and the remaining articles talk in terms of "the as-yet-unfulfilled promise of the historic turn" (Mills et al., 2016, p. 74). Of the latter grouping of papers only McCann (2016) discusses the historic turn at any length, arguing that even "within its own narrow terms it is still ongoing rather than achieved" (quoted in Mills et al., 2016, p. 74). McCann contends that a realization of the historic turn will require that "much of the folk wisdom about people and corporations – and indeed about "history" itself – is likely to be revised" (Ibid.). This led Mills et al. (2016) to conclude that they could not "attest to the claim . . . that a historic turn is underway in MOS" (Mills et al., 2016, p. 71). They could, however, surmise that Booth and Rowlinson's (2006) article influenced the development of "theoretically and methodologically rich and varied approaches to history" (Mills et al., 2016, p. 71). This was largely evidenced by the fact that the articles in the Special Issue drew on ANTi-History (Corrigan, 2016; Marshall & Novicevic, 2016; Poor, Novicevic, Humphreys, & Popooola, 2016), Rhetorical History (Poor et al., 2016; Smith & Russell, 2016; Zundel et al., 2016), Foucauldian genealogy (Marshall & Novicevic, 2016; Poor et al., 2016), social memory theory (Marshall & Novicevic, 2016; Poor et al., 2016), Bourdieu's critical sociology (Carson, Carson, & Phillips, 1997), career narratives (McCann, 2016), Goffman's dramaturgy (Corrigan, 2016), "polyphonic constitutive historicism" (Smith & Russell, 2016) and path dependence (Brunninge & Melander, 2016).

Special Issues in *M&OH*

One of several important outcomes of the call for a HT has been to encourage new ways of looking at history, the past, and the relationship between them. In the case of established methodological approaches (e.g., feminism, postmodernism) within the discipline of History, Booth and Rowlinson call for a recovery/rediscovery of those approaches for business and management history. They contend that "calls for more historical awareness are often aligned with critical management studies" (p. 7). Here they cite Zald's and Burrell's contentions that business studies have been "cut off from humanistic thinking," and Jacques argument is that "an historical perspective" can "provide a critically reflective vision of the good society" (p. 7). Booth and Rowlinson (2006, pp. 7–8) go on to argue that "the historic turn also involves more critical and ethical reflection," including a rewriting of race, gender, sexuality, and postcoloniality (pp. 7–8). In the last regard, they example the work of Anshuman Prasad, who "seeks to theorize workplace diversity within the wider context of the (continuing?) history and experience of Euro-American imperialism and colonialism" (Booth & Rowlinson, 2006, p. 8). To what extent new (e.g., ANTi-History) and recovered methodologies (e.g., gender studies, feminism, and postcolonialism) have been taken up within management and organizational history (MOH) is the focus of the next sections, beginning with feminism, postcolonialism, and postmodernism.

Feminism

In 2010 Mary Phillips and Ann Rippin co-edited a Special Issue of *M&OH*, titled "Women in Management and Organizational History."[3] Here Phillips and Rippin (2010) noted that there was "little if any work taking place on the part played by women in the construction of management practices" (p. 283). Thus, drawing on feminist theory, they set out to articulate a desire "to speak in the name of women; of women's experiences, subjectivities and sexualities, claiming 'a language of our own' and 'a history of our own'" (p. 283). Alongside the all-important notions of "reclaiming women in management and organization history" (p. 283), the Special Issue challenged the role of gender and gender politics in how authorship is privileged through such things as organizational focus (e.g., male-dominated work) and the exclusion of non-paid work from the study of organizing and managing (Phillips, 2010, p. 296; Phillips & Rippin, 2010, p. 286). Several contributions to the issue detail and challenge the marginalization of women's work and of the role of women in history, including the marginalization of female management theorists and historians (Hannam, 2010; Holden, 2010; Hopfl, 2010; Phillips, 2010; Rehn & Rippin, 2010, Sanderson, Parsons, Helms Mills, & Mills, 2010; Wall, 2010).[4]

History in translation

A review of three selected[5] management history journals – *Management & Organizational History*; the *Journal of Management History*, and *Business History* – strongly supports Phillips and Rippin's (2010) argument about the neglect of gender and feminist studies in the field.[6] Between mid-2006 and mid-2010, when the MOH special issue on women in history was published, the number of female authors ranged from just over 17 per cent to just under 28 per cent (see Table 5.1). The situation was not much improved in the period since the publication of the special issue (see Table 5.2). To begin with, the over total of female authors fell as did the percentages for *Business History* and the *Journal of Management History*. The only increase was in the number of female authors publishing in *Management & Organizational History* but this may also be due to the sheer number of female authors (13) that were drawn to publish in the special issue, which in itself says something about the gendered dynamics of publishing.

Table 5.1 Percentage of female authors in three leading management history journals, 2006–2010

Journal	No. of articles[a]	No. of authors[b]	No. (%) of female authors
BH	233	281	67 (23.8)
M&OH	93	144	25 (17.3)
JMH	94	169	47 (27.8)
Totals	420	594	139 (23.4)

a This includes book reviews by named reviewers.
b This refers to a simple name count for each article rather than a count of the different number of *individual* authors. Thus, for example, Ann Rippin's name appears on several articles and each mention counts as a female author. This means that there are many fewer individual female authors than may be indicated.

Table 5.2 Percentage of female authors in three leading management history journals, 2011–2018

Journal	No. of articles	No. of authors	No. (%) female authors
BH	758	1,143	200 (17.5)
M&OH	193	314	84 (26.7)
JMH	229	459	101 (22)
Totals	1,180	1,916	385 (21)

Female authorship is only one measure of the gendered dynamics of publishing and should not be taken to represent gender studies, women's history, or feminist methodologies (but most of the female authors of the 2010 special issue did deal with gender and women's histories as well as draw on feminist research). Examining the numerous articles (1600) published in BH, JMH and MOH between 2006 and the end of 2018 we found very few that dealt with either feminist research and/or women's history, but there were some exceptions – discussed below.

The earliest article we can find for this period (2006–2018) appeared in a 2009 issue of *Journal of Management History (JMH)* by Jennifer Oyler and Mildred Golden Pryor (2009). In their analysis of Peter Drucker's contribution to workplace diversity, Oyler and Pryor liken the neglect of Drucker's role to the treatment of female management theorists, arguing that:

Because [Mary Parker Follett's] assumptions did not fit the realities which the budding discipline of management assumed in the

1930s and 1940s, she became a "nonperson" even before her death in 1932, with her work practically forgotten for 25 years or more. And yet we now know that her basic assumptions regarding society, people and management were far closer to reality than those on which the management people then based themselves – and still largely base themselves today.

(p. 421)

Nonetheless, the article is almost wholly focused on the work of Peter Drucker and reference to Mary Parker Follett was limited to an example only.[7] However, discussion of Mary Parker Follett appeared in a more in-depth analysis in a 2011 issue of *JMH*. In "Mary, Mary, quite contrary," Simone T.A. Phipps (2011) sought to recover women's voice in arguing that "in a male-dominated field, women contributed by bringing a touch of spirituality to early management theory and practice" (p. 270). Her work encourages a revisiting of the impact of Mary Parker Follett and Mary Barnett Gilson on the development of management studies, as well as the inclusion of "spirituality" as a focus of historical accounts. She didn't have to wait long. Two years later *JMH* published three articles on Parker Follett in its 19.4 issue. The first – by Milorad Novicevic, John Humphreys, M. Roland Buckley, Foster Roberts, and Andrew Hebdon (2013) – drew on the work of Parker Follett to offer "unique practical recommendations for instructional methods of experiential learning." The second – by Jane Whitney Gibson – examined "significant contributions of Follett through the lens of critical biography to put her work in the context of her life events, her mentors, and the other major influences on her work" (p. 441). Gibson describes her critical biography approach as a qualitative method with which social historians research the individual scholar's or practitioner's critical incidents in life in order to explore and explain the subject's scholarly development and intellectual contributions, situated in the social and historical background of the subject" (p. 441). In the third article Sébastien Damart (2013) analyses "Follett's way of reasoning" (p. 459) to reveal how she influenced the development of management theory.[8]

In similar fashion the marginalization of Frances Perkins is the focus of two articles in *JMH* (Prieto, Phipps, Thompson, Lemaro, & Smith, 2016; Williams & Mills, 2017). The first of the two "examines the contributions made by [Perkins and other] notable women through the lens of stakeholder theory and the feminist ethic of care" (Prieto et al., 2016, p. 50), while the second uses "a feminist poststructural lens" to address the neglect of Perkins in MOS and reveal her potential contributions to the field (Williams & Mills, 2017, p. 32). The authors describe their feminist poststructuralist approach as "focus on major discourses (dominant interrelated practices and ideas) that influence how people come to define themselves, others and the character of a particular phenomenon (e.g. management history)" (Williams & Mills, 2017, p. 32). This involves the examination of various sources "that collectively work to present a dominant idea of a given set of practices (in this case, management and organization studies and associated histories of the field)" (p. 32).[9]

In an earlier study Prieto (2012) reported on the role of gender dynamics in the production of psychological knowledge.[10] Here he studied the impact of Hugo Munsterberg's "chauvinistic opinions" on "the lives of his students, some of whom were feminists" (Prieto, 2012, p. 166). In the process Prieto focuses on Munsterberg's students: Mary Calkins, Ethel Puffer, and William Marsden "who went on to make valuable contributions in psychology, women's issues, the polygraph, and the creation of the first and most famous comic book super heroine" (p. 166). In a similar vein Hartt, Helms Mills, and Mills (2012) who, in the study of a teachers' union, analyse "the role of history in the creation of gender dynamics" (p. 82). Here Hartt et al. explore how present-day gender politics influenced the eventual "degendered" history of the foundation of the union (p. 94).

More recently Williams and Mills (2018) examined the neglect of Hattie Flanagan in MOS, calling for a rethink of the field definition of both MOS and MOH by focusing on issues of social welfare and creativity in studies of organizing and managing.

In the lead up to the *M&OH* Special Issue on Women's History there had been little in the way of women's or feminist history in *JMH*, *BH* (*Business History*), and *M&OH*. With the exception of a brief comment in Oyler and Pryor (2019), there had been only three references in *BH* – all book reviews and focused on "enterprising women." The first was a review of "Enterprising women and shipping in the nineteenth century" by Helen Doe and reviewed by Sheryllynne Haggerty. Haggerty (2010) opines that "Doe wants to present her women not as "dependent victims" (p. 1), but as active agents within a difficult world" (p. 342). Then, proclaiming herself as "a proponent of a 'positive past' for women's history myself," Haggerty goes on to express her pleasure at seeing "such an approach taken here," concluding that "Doe pulls this off nicely" (p. 342). The second review, by Hans-Heinrich Nolte (2010), reports on Galina Ulianova's book on "Female entrepreneurs in nineteenth-century Russia." Despite the fact that the book raises issues about equal rights, the reviewer says nothing about women's history or feminist historiography. The third reviewer, Katrina Honeyman, opens with a stinging rebuke of the field of business history for its "enduring gender blindness" that defies rational explanation (Honeyman, 2010, p. 340). In support of Alison Kay's book on "female enterprise in 19th-century London," Honeyman contends that Kay's "important scholarship contributes to women's history." Nonetheless, she cautions, despite this research, "the myth of women's entrepreneurial insignificance persists" (Honeyman, 2010, p. 340).

Of a total of 15 items published in *BH* between mid-2006 and the end of 2018 almost half (7) were book reviews. One is interesting in drawing attention to how the author's (Emma Robertson) study of "chocolate, women and empire" focuses on how "the cultural construction of chocolate in marketing has relied on and produced hegemonic narratives of gender, class, race and empire" (Murillo, 2009, p. 471) – especially, the author's exploration of "how Western control of global markets has exploited people and resources in the global South" (Murillo, 2009, p. 471). The remaining three book reviews focus on comparisons between men and women in regard to finance. This is also the focus of one of the eight articles. Insights from the remaining *BH* articles include a focus on the role of masculinity on occupational identity (van den Broek, 2011), gender ideology (Eriksson, 2014), U.S. corporate strategies and gender in Brazil (Moura, 2015), inequality and workplace value (Crowley, 2016), women's contributions to Swedish family business (Nordlund Edvinsson, 2015), gender history (Arnberg & Svanlund, 2016), and narrating histories of women at work (Durepos et al., 2017). The last paper exemplifies the type of discussion that Booth and Rowlinson (2006) envisioned as an outcome of their critical call. Durepos et al. (2017) contend that "narrative is constructed in the historical research process, with implications for our understanding of business history as product and practice." They go on to "suggest that business historians work with a distinction between stories in description, generated by participants as found in traces of the past, and narration through analysis, created by historians writing in the present." Recognizing this distinction may encourage business historians may be "better able to consider the position of women in both forms of narrative" (p. 1).

In contrast to the number of articles and book reviews on gender and history published in *BH* we could only find seven in *JMH* (reviewed above) and seven[11] in *M&OH*. The earliest of the *M&OH* articles appeared in a 2007 issue, authored by Mary Phillips, focused on a "17th century gendered turf war between midwives and medics" (Phillips, 2007). The second article appeared shortly after the 2010 Special Issue and set out to reclaim Lillian Gilbreth's "position in the history of management thought" (Krenn, 2011). The third appeared in a Special Issue on "Theorizing the Past: Critical Engagements" and explored "the relationship between current gendered practices and past conditions through the lens of actor-network theory" (Corrigan & Mills, 2012, p. 251). Through a case study of gender politics in Air Canada's board room, the authors contend that ANT and feminist theory can be reconciled through "identifying and surfacing" how combinations of human and non-human actors combine to work within networks that "produce gendered effects" such as discriminatory practices (Corrigan & Mills, p. 251). The fourth article appeared in 2013. Authored by Anna Kuokkanen and Hannele Seeck, the article set out to study the influence of masculinity that is embedded within organizational culture and serves as subtle resistance to the introduction of new management ideas that do not conform to the cultural values. The fifth and six articles both appeared in 2018. The first of these two is by Caterina Bettin and Albert Mills, who set out to offer "an account of the complexity of the 'subject of the past'" in a case study of Simone de Beauvoir. Centrally, a methodological article, Bettin and Mills propose "a multiple and relational approach to the construction of the subjects of the past" and demonstrate the use of the approach in evaluating de Beauvoir's potential contribution to MOS (Bettin & Mills, 2018, p. 65). The sixth and final article takes up some of the same theoretical threads of Bettin and Mills (2018) in an amodernist account of the making of a commercial airline. Here, Nicholous Deal, Albert J. Mills, and Jean Helms Mills draw on ANTi-History (Durepos & Mills, 2012a) and microhistory (Magnússon & Szijártó, 2013) to "examine how wartime experience prior, during, and following World War I came to shape the development of gendered organizational processes and practices in Imperial Airways' emergent organizational culture from 1924–1939" (Deal, Mills & Helms Mills, 2018, p. 373).

Summary

Our review of three major journals in the field of business, management, and organizational history only revealed 29 articles (including 7 book reviews) from a total of 1,600 published between 2006 and the end of 2018. That is less than two percent of the total. Even then several of the articles had little to say about gender, feminism, or women's history. Very few dealt at any length with the contribution of women's history, gender and history, and/or feminist approaches to history. But perhaps this is not surprising as the field of MOS itself continues to be taken to task for ignoring gender (Calás, Smircich, & Holvino, 2014; Hearn et al., 2015; Mills, 2017). The articles we included in our review were chosen to illustrate the types of issue and methodologies that could contribute to ongoing debates within MOH and open the field to a range of new and different ideas. Disappointingly, as we shall see in the next section, issues of race, diversity, and postcoloniality feature even less than do articles dealing with gender.

Race to the post: postcoloniality and management history

In this section we looked through 1,600 articles for ones that centrally dealt with race and/or postcolonial studies. We found 12 (0.75%) that could be roughly divided into those focused on African-American business and management history (4) and those that focused on post-colonial theory (8). Four articles were published in *JMH*, six in *M&OH*, and two in *BH*. In the latter case both were book reviews of histories of African-American business in the USA (Bristol, 2010) that con-tribute "much to the developing historiography of African-American entrepreneurship" (Willett, 2011, p. 469). Two articles dealing with African-American influences on management theory appeared in *JMH* in 2012 and in 2016. In both cases the focus was on uncover-ing the influence of two specific African-American men – Benjamin Montgomery ("a former slave who eventually became manager and, ultimately, owner of the Hurricane plantation" – Jones, Novicevic, Hayek, & Humphreys, 2012, p. 46) and Charles Clinton Spaulding ("a prominent black business leader in the USA in the early 1900s" – Prieto & Phipps, 2016, p. 73). The thoughts of both men were accessi-ble through their writings and reflections, uncovered through archival research.

Serving as a kind of bridge between African-American manage-ment and postcolonial theory is a *JMH* article that examines the in-fluence of Ibn Khaldun on North Africa, a 14th-century philosopher and historian, who is said to have made important, but ignored, con-tributions to leadership theory (Sidani, 2008). To be clear, the author does not draw on postcolonial theories. Nonetheless, we have included the article here because it was a rare discussion in *JMH* on the mar-ginalization of non-Western ideas. A final *JMH* article that deals specifically with postcolonial theory[12] is Nimruji Jammulamadaka's study of "the roots of business-society relationships in India and its contribution to postcolonial perspectives on corporate responsibility" (2016, p. 450). Through an archival study of Bombay textile mills in the late 19th and early 20th centuries, Jammulamadaka demonstrates that "the evolution of business–society relations in a post-colonial context shows how they are different from the Western trajectory" (p. 450). Namely,

> postcolonial accounts of CSR history can only be understood as emerging from a triadic interaction of imperial interest, subordinated native business and native societal relationships. This contrasts with conventional [Western] approaches that look at CSR's emergence simply as a process internal to that society.
>
> (Ibid.)

The final eight, *M&OH*, articles all involve postcolonial and de-colonial perspectives (i.e., revealing suppressed local knowledges and realities and elevating "voices from the South"). As we shall see, two of the three articles engage directly with the HT.

One of the articles we included because the authors – Sluyterman and Bouwens (2015) – explore the impact of the Heineken brewery on "colonial empires and developing countries." They do not, however, draw on either postcolonial studies or de-colonial theory.

The first of the three postcolonial studies is by Nidhi Srinivas (2010) who undertakes a post-colonial reading of Walter Benjamin's "Theses on the Philosophy of History." Srinivas' reading draws on postcolonial historians Sanjay Subrahmanyam and Rajnarayan Chandavarkar. He goes on to explore the different ways in which Benjamin's work and postcolonial histories reveal a profound under-theorization of the past in current debates around fusions of history and organization studies. This provides a nod towards the debate around the HT, but it remains little more than an echo in his discussion of Benjamin. In the second paper Sara Louise Muhr and Azad Salem (2013) draw on postcolonial theory to study the impact of "specters of colonialism" on a Swedish organization, to reveal "the role that European colonial history has played" in the shaping of national identities of countries not normally associated with colonialism (p. 62). In the "silence of the archives" Stefanie Decker (2013), in our third paper, sets out using post-colonial theory to show the problems and challenges of drawing on archives that were developed in former British colonies. She contends that historical methodology should take into account postcolonial influences on archival developments.

The issue of the HT is more centrally engaged with in the following two articles. The first draws on the contrasting fates of two leading business historians, Alfred Chandler (USA), whose work made him globally famous, and Celso Furtado (Brazil), who was largely unknown outside of Latin America. Here Sergio Wanderley and Alex Faria (2012) draw on de-colonial theory to explain the processes of how certain knowledges (e.g., voices from the South) get suppressed and marginalized. In the process, they introduced us to several keys terms to explore "how a decolonial framework can inform management and organizational knowledge (MOK) with the objective of fostering a decolonized historic turn (HT) agenda from Latin America" (Wanderley & Faria, 2012, p. 219). To that end, our attention is drawn to several key terms from de-colonial thinking, including *"locus of enunciation"* – a historical perspective that is shaped by the broad context (usually "the North") in which certain ideas dominate; *"multipolar"* – knowledge that is co-produced from various locations; *"pluriversality"* – the processes through which different knowledges come to co-exist, thus several knowledges rather than a singular, universal knowledge; and *"border thinking"* – a metaphorical space where new knowledge can emerge from encounters of the modern and the colonial, providing voice to the formerly colonized to pursue the generation of pluriversality. Applying this to the HT, Wanderley and Faria (2012, p. 224) adopt a de-colonial perspective to embrace it *"in a particular way"* (our emphasis). To that end, they critically engage with "authors of the North" who have problematized the spread of management knowledge in the USA during the Cold War but have underplayed the role of coloniality. Thus, Wanderley and Faria (2012, p. 219) seek to "create conditions for the development of a multipolar and pluriversal field of strategy . . . which moves beyond the North/South divide."

In the third article, Wanderley, with Amon Barros, returns to the issue of de-coloniality and the geopolitics of knowledge through an in-depth analysis of the HT. They begin by clarifying their de-colonial, in contrast to a postcolonial, perspective. They contend that both perspectives are complementary in striving to "unveil colonial strategies, promoting the reproduction of subjects whose aims and goals are to control" (Wanderley & Barros, 2018, p. 81). However, they differ in their origins, with postcolonial studies rooted largely in the colonization experience of India and de-colonization rooted in the Latin American experience. Simply put, the different experiences of colonialism have shaped different forms of postcoloniality, leading to different engagements between colonized and colonizer and different "concepts, objects and themes of investigation" (p. 82). Wanderley and Barros (2018, p. 82) go on to contend that postcolonial studies "continue to work with Western-derived epistemology and categories of analysis" (p. 82) and, in contrast to border thinking, "the provenance of postcolonial thinking is profoundly Eurocentric" (p. 84).

Moving on to analysis of the HT, Wanderley and Barros (2018) explore "how a decolonial framework can inform MOK [management and organizational knowledge] with the objective of fostering a decolonized historic turn (HT) agenda from Latin America" (p. 79). Here Wanderley and Barros (2018) focus on Booth and Rowlinson (2006) as a starting point for their critique, which they develop through a series of arguments. They begin by asking "whether the dominance of Anglo-Saxon knowledge has become any different with the introduction of the HT in MOK . . . [and] whether the HT has opened space for introduction of theories, authors, concepts, objects, and themes from other spaces as well (p. 80). They answer a clear "no," arguing that the HT "has not promoted the inclusion of Latin America in the house of knowledge" (p. 93); that "theories of organization should not only be criticized for being ahistorical (Booth & Rowlinson, 2006), but also for missing a geographical orientation since they take for granted the Anglo-Saxon world is the sole source of theory" (Ibarra-Colado, 2006, 2008, p. 80); and that "together with a historic turn we must introduce a geographic turn in MOK to include other spaces in order to promote a shift in the geography of reasoning" (p. 93).

Wanderley and Barros (2018) critique the HT from several vantage points, turning certain arguments back on the HT. For example, "HT falls into the trap of being 'told from the Western perspective, as if there were a single, linear, and ascending history in time and a single center in space'" (p. 80) – embracing "a Western time line that suppresses space under the domination of time" (p. 81); that "HT posited by the center falls into its own critique of 'presentism' (Booth & Rowlinson, 2006 6) since it remains in the extended past of the domination of Anglo-Saxon knowledge" (p. 81); and that the "HT may also fall prey to its own critique of universalism (Booth & Rowlinson, 2006 6)" (p. 81). In summary, Wanderley and Barros (2018, p. 81) argue that their critiques "may lead to another one, namely, neocolonialism . . . since authors from Latin America and themes from this area almost never appear in these debates" (p. 81).[13]

Summary

As we have discussed above, there have been even fewer papers dealing with race and postcolonialism than those dealing with gender and feminism in our three selected journals. This is compounded by the fact that only one of the race/postcolonial papers also deal with gender/feminism. The exception is Jammulamadaka (2016), who deals at length with women's work in a postcolonial environment. Similarly, only one of the gender/feminism papers deals with either race or post-coloniality. Here the exception is the book review of "chocolate, women and empire" (Murillo, 2011).[14] We also observe that only two papers – Wanderley & Faria (2012) and Wanderley & Barros (2018) – directly discuss the impact of the HT on management and organizational studies. This provides some other interesting clues to the production of historical accounts and what gets privileged and what gets marginalized. As Wanderley and Barros (2018, p. 82) suggest, "had [they] presented themselves as 'Foucauldians or [the] actor networkers' it would certainly have made [them] more attractive critters[15] to the audiences in the Global North." And they reflect that

> from the locus of enunciation of Latin America, we must ask ourselves whether engaging with the Anglo-Saxon HT makes us part of the group of 'proud critical (or advanced) thinkers', who, in fact, do not recognize the extent to which they are Eurocentric . . .

It is also a useful segue to our next section on the rise of postmodernist historiography in MOS and the development of new forms of historiography – specifically ANTi-History and Rhetorical History.

Thoroughly post-modern

As discussed earlier, in 2004 Rowlinson outlined what he saw as three key historical perspectives in organization studies – the factual, the narrative, and the archaeo-genealogical; the latter largely refers to Foucauldian analyses. Arguably, Rowlinson was not merely describing these approaches but actually making a case for each of them to be viewed as a legitimate approach to the study of the past. Returning to our three management history journals, a word search of key words that included Foucault, postmodern*, poststructural*, and histor* yielded 48 articles dealing with postmodernist approaches to history.[16] We found references to postmodern history in 10 *JMH* papers, 12 *BH* papers, and 26 *M&OH* papers. By and large, although somewhat distanced from postmodernism (Mordhorst & Schwarzkopf, 2017), if not out-and-out opposed (Kroeze & Keulen, 2013), the papers in *BH* tended to engage in a way that views postmodernism as being an important approach to history (Usdiken & Kieser, 2004) that business historians should interact with (Decker, Kipping, & Wadhwani, 2015). Indeed, as early as 2004 Usdiken & Kieser were contending that postmodernist perspectives "have had a significant influence, in the last decade or so on management and organisation studies, especially outside North

America" (p. 325). Critiques of postmodernism include "overemphasis on relativism, polyphony and deconstruction" and "the tendency to view everything as text" (Kroeze & Keulen, 2013, p. 1270).

The papers published in *JMH* seem more or less sharply divided between critique (e.g., Bowden, 2016) and application (e.g., Kemp, 2013). In the latter case, Kemp sets out to show the use value of post-modernism through the deconstruction of four principles of scientific management (p. 345). Bowden (2016), on the other hand, sets up his critique by arguing that the role of management theory is to produce research that "leads to better organisations, institutions, workplaces, economies and social relationships." The research should be con-ducted in ways that are "based around the testing of research theses," and consistent with "management history's methodological bedrock" (p. 118). However, he concludes, "the growth of postmodernist and poststructuralist research paradigms [far from meeting this criteria] has created uncertainty with regards to both methods and purpose among management and business historians" (Bowden, 2016, p. 118). Other critiques include the argument that postmodern management authors "are not merely suspicious of a science of management . . . they dismiss it altogether" (Joullié, 2018, p. 385). Such scholars, Joullié (2018, p. 390) continues, "escape the charge of determinism but face that of theoretical paralysis and practical irrelevance."

Most of the articles that are favourably produced from a postmod-ernist perspective appear in *M&OH*. In the very first issue of the jour-nal Alan McKinlay (2006, p. 87) sets out to "draw attention to the centrality of the body of Foucault's work" for business historians. Over succeeding years, various authors drew on postmodernist theory to make sense of archival research (McKinlay, 2013); to problematize "methodological realism" (Weatherbee, 2012); as a means of integrat-ing history and organization studies (Decker, 2016; Miskell, 2018); the influence of postmodern architecture on ways of thinking, corporate identities, and the "changing symbolic, economic and social power of such corporations in the period 1945–2005" (Kerr, Robinson, & Elliott, 2016, p. 140).

Summary

Searching through *BH*, *JMH*, and *M&OH* it is clear that some space has been opened to postmodernist approaches to history since 2006. However, that space has not so much opened in terms of the sheer numbers of postmodernist articles published in those journals but in terms of a kind of normalization and legitimization of postmodern history (Usdiken & Kieser, 2004; Decker, 2016). The publication of around 48 articles out of 1,600 (3%) can hardly be seen as a HT. Indeed, a majority of the 48 articles are more dismissive than accepting. Nonetheless, it is fair to say that postmodernist accounts are, regardless of Bowden's (2016) dismissal, being treated as a part of the landscape of MOH.

New turns and developments

Part of Booth and Rowlinson's (2006) call for a HT was the expressed hope that organizational historians would search for new ways of dealing with the past and history. Searching through the management history journals there are various signs of newly "borrowed approaches" from the field of history (e.g., postmodernism) as well as newly developed approaches (e.g., ANTi-History) through engagement with History. Notable among these are *feminism*, *postmodernism*, *de-colonialism*, and *postcolonial theory* (discussed at length above), as well as "*neuro-scientific management*" (Corbett, 2008; "*critical realist*" *historiography* (Clark & Blundel, 2007); "*Bourdieu's theory of practice*" (Lyke, 2017); "*conceptual history*" (Andersen, 2011; Costea, Crumpt, & Holm, 2006); "*historical cultural approach*" (Crump, Ameridis, & Costea, 2007); "*Counter factual history*" (Maielli, 2007); "*genealogical pragmatic analysis*" (Marshall & Novicevic, 2016; Poor et al., 2016); "*path dependence*" (Mordhorst, 2008, 2014; Schreyogg, Sydow, & Holtmann, 2011); Mordhorst and Schwarzkopf (2017); "*ANTi-History*" (Corrigan, 2016; Corrigan & Mills, 2012; Durepos, Mills, & Weatherbee, 2012; Pfefferman, 2017); "*Rhetorical History*" (Foster, Coraiola, Suddaby, Kroezen & Chandler, 2017; Foster, Suddaby, Minkus, & Weibe, 2011; Lubinski, 2018; Smith & Simeone, 2017); "*Counter narrative history*" (Mordhorst, 2008); "*microhistory*" (MacLean, Harvey, & Clegg, 2015; MacLean, Harvey, Sillince & Golant, 2014); "*neo-institutionalist history*" (Rowlinson & Hassard, 2013; Suddaby, Foster & Mills, 2014); "*social movement theory*" (MacLean et al., 2015); "*Critical hermeneutics*" (Taylor, Bell, & Cooke, 2009; Toms & Wilson, 2010); "*evolutionary theory*" (Quinn, 2015); "*ethnomethodology*" (Whittle & Wilson, 2015); "*polyphonic constitutive historicism*" (Smith & Russell, 2016); Ricoeurian (Taylor et al., 2009) and Benjaminesque perspectives on history (Rippin, 2013; Srinivas, 2010); and likely several other approaches that we have missed in our sweep of management history journals and special issues on a HT in MOS.

In reviewing new turns and developments, Mills et al. (2016) singled out two approaches – ANTi-History and Rhetorical History.[17]

The first was developed in 2008 with a paper that traced networks of human (e.g., company executives) and non-human (e.g., transcripts of interviews with employees) actors in the production of a history of Pan American Airways (Durepos et al., 2008). It is:

> an approach that through critical engagement with both history and organizational analysis seeks to understand knowledge of the past, extant knowledge and the interactions of the two through studies of the relational networks that constituted them. "From this perspective history becomes important as an artifact of heterogeneous relations [of] human and non-human actors working in concert . . . that produces the idea of history and the specifics of any claim to historical relevance. Similarly, organizational knowledge is viewed as the outcome of heterogeneous relations that is somehow mediated by knowledge of the past-as-history (Munslow, 2015) and its links to heterogeneous relations."
>
> (Mills et al., 2016, p. 70)

Studies using ANTi-History include Myrick, Helms Mills and Mills (2013) tracing of a dominant history of the Academy of Management and the implications for academic evaluations; Coller et al.'s (2016) study of the development of the British Airways Heritage and archive collection and its impact of histories of the airline; Hartt, Mills, Helms Mills and Corrigan's (2014) study of the role of history as a "non-corporeal actant" in Air Canada's executive leadership succession; and Novicevic et al.'s (2019) study of said enforcement and contestation of Meredith's leadership of racial integration at the University of Mississippi.

Over a similar time span there has been growing interest in Rhetorical History (associated with Roy Suddaby and Bill Foster). This involves study of "the process of using historical discourse for strategic purposes":

> The concept of rhetorical history draws from ongoing historiographic debates about the epistemological status of narration in history and successful challenges to claims of objectivity in history raised by post-structuralist (Foucault, 1980), interpretive (White, 1973), feminist (Lerner, 1986) and Marxist (Hobsbawn, 1997) historians. In contrast to traditional history, which seems to understand the past in historical context, rhetorical history seeks to understand the past from a 'presentist' point of view . . .
>
> When viewed with a specific focus on understanding how we talk about the past in the present, history is recognised less as

an objective fact and more as a highly valuable and malleable re-source that, increasingly, is used by organizations for strategic purposes.

(Mills et al., 2016, pp. 70–71)

Paradigm shift: from popular front to fragmentation?

As we saw above earliest paper on a call for a HT engaged the ire of some unknown Academy of Management reviewer who was unhappy with their argument that "most business historians [are] common sense empiricists." This contributed to a rejection of the paper, likely to the view that it was irrelevant to management and business history. Nonetheless, within six years, the idea of injecting more history into MOS seems to have captured the imagination of various people in the broad field of history that focused on business, management, and organizational history work. The *JMH* was revived as a largely positivist, or factualist independent journal alongside the foundation of the new and broadly critical *Management & Organizational Studies*. Several conference sessions across various associations attracted both positivist and critical historians, and the era saw various special issues of scholarly journals, including *Human Relations* (2006),[18] *M&OH* (2012),[19] *Organization* (2014),[20] *M&OH* (2016),[21] *AMR*[22] *Organization Studies* (2018),[23] and a few others. A simple review of the editors and authors involved reveals a relatively eclectic group of scholars across various paradigms; in an earlier political era, this group might be referred to as a united or popular front. In large part this may have had to do with the hoped for outcome of an actual HT in MOS, with historians playing an important and sometime key role.

There were, of course, debates over the years but they rarely rose to the level of a skirmish. An early debate, between Alfred Kieser and Paul Goldman (see Chapter 3), may have come close to a skirmish where Goldman endeavoured to reduce historians to "myopic fact-collectors without a method." This blanket characterization may have served to garner support for Kieser, especially from those otherwise engaged with the past from a different historical perspective. Early on one gets the impression that positivist-oriented historians of the factual kind (Rowlinson, 2004) tended to be more dismissive of postmodernist historians than intellectually angered. Being more or less excluded from the field, postmodernist historians seemed at first to have a need to provide a defence of their approach and/or to critique positivist accounts. In the event, it would appear that, for the most part, the positivist historians rarely took the bait as postmodernism became somewhat normalized in business, management, and organizational history. Or so we thought . . .!

One formally constructed debate over 2009–2010, which was initiated by Scott Taylor, Emma Bell, and Bill Cooke (2009) who argued that "there is little sign of reflexive historiography within business history, and suggest the reluctance goes some way towards explaining the sub-discipline's relative isolation from the rest of organization and management studies" (p. 151). These authors then draw on the work of Ricoeur to encourage business historians to reflect more on the processes of constructing historical narratives, concluding that more "reflective engagement with the foundations and products of the historiographical operation would help to make the conduct of history less tacit and therefore more comprehensible to non-historians, and thus more difficult to marginalize or dismiss" (p. 164). Reflecting on their own writing style, Scott et al. (2009, p. 164) go on to recognize that their article had "been written in a deliberately provocative tone."

Responding to the provocation, Steve Toms and John Wilson (2010) offer a detailed reply but state early on that Taylor et al.'s (2009) "critique is constructive and to be welcomed as contributing to a debate about the future of business history, and especially its relationship with organisation studies" (Toms & Wilson, 2010, p. 109). They then launch a critique that (i) Taylor et al.'s (2019) recommended adoption of a specific epistemological position as a necessary condition for conducting business history is unsustainable; (ii) "relativist epistemological positions . . . . potentially undermine the output of business historians by casting unnecessary doubt on the credibility of their claims arising from empirical results"; (iii) Taylor et al. (2019) present an uncritical characterization of Ricoeur's work that contains "logical inconsistencies and potentially serious methodological problems"; and (iv) Taylor et al. (2019) unfairly blame *Business History* and business historians carrying "responsibility for the disjuncture between business history and organisation studies" (Toms & Wilson, 2010, p. 109).

More recently debate has taken on a sharper tone. In 2017 Stephen Cummings, Todd Bridgman, John Hassard, and Mick Rowlinson teamed up to produce "A New History of Management." In many ways this book stands in sharp contrast to the main U.S. management text books over the years by Claude George (1968, 1972), Daniel Wren (1972, 1979), Art Bedeian (1986), and Wren and Bedeian (2009, 2018).

To start with, as if a nod to Bowden's (2016) argument about the role of management research to lead "to better organisations, institutions, workplaces, economies and social relationships" (p. 118), Cummings et al. (2017) contend that "rather than seeking innovation . . . by running away from the past, we can, instead, seek innovation by looking more deeply at our interpretations of the past and how these limit our horizons" (p. xii). They describe this approach as "counter history" (p. xiii) and, building on the work of Foucault, construct the book around "Six Counter-Historical Strategies" (p. 41) as follows[24]:

1   "**Move from linear time as a model for history to space** . . ." With history arising out of the juxtaposition of abrupt differences rather than the outcome of a smooth progression of ideas."
2   Assess time periods not as chronological progress but rather "in line with **the conditions in which human beings 'problematize'** existence."
3   "Examine how **object and subject co-determine one another**" rather than treat them as separate entities.
4   "Focus on how **objects/subjects are constituted by** . . . [a] **web of relations**."
5   "**Overturn accepted continuities and discontinuities** in conventional historical narratives."
6   Challenge conventional histories through raising **doubts and alternatives** rather than seeking objective or real truths.

Cummings et al. (2017, p. 34) see these strategies as being in "parallel with an emerging historic, or historical, turn in organization and management studies" alongside "a cultural or critical turn in management history."

In the year following publication of "A New History of Management" (New History), Bradley Bowden launched his own book-length critique, "Work, Wealth, & Postmodernism" (WWP). This was at least his second critique, following on from his editorial in the *JMH* (see Bowden, 2016). This has been followed by a further critique in the form of a guest editorial in the journal *Qualitative Research in Organizations and Management* (QROM) called "Empiricism, Epistemology and Modern Postmodernism: A Critique."[25] Alongside this article there is a rebuttal article by Simon Mollan (in press); two further articles that broadly support Bowden's position appeared early in 2019 (Batiz-Lazo, 2019; Muldoon, 2018); and a further Special Issue of current debates on management history in the *JMH*[26] in the first half of 2020.

In sharp contrast to Cummings et al.'s (2017) focus on how to make sense of history and the past (viz. historical method), Bowden focuses on the personal and the political importance of history. In the first case, he is referring to the hard-won experiences and subsequent stories of class and material progress that inhabited his family's narratives. In the second case, he "seeks to defend what once needed no defence: the modern world with its universities, its immense wealth, and its deeply ingrained traditions of democracy and respect for individual rights" (p. vi).

In these two examples we likely glean a sense of the passion that fuels his critique. However, some of this is quite troubling in its apparently over-emphasis on the need to guard against attacks "not only [on] modernity but also the entire structure of Western language and thought" (p. 12). Yet, in fairness, he states elsewhere that "it is difficult to not to be attracted by claims that 'emancipatory potential . . . lies in questioning the ethnocentricity' of current Western knowledge and scholarship."[27] Nonetheless, he deals with this critique by arguing that postmodernism "is a false prophet . . . [because] postmodernists have chosen to abjure economics . . . thereby marginalizing themselves in the debates about wealth creation and economic policy that remain central to our world" (pp. 17–18).

Along the way Bowden takes on various other aspects of postmodernism that include, what he terms, "the postmodernist assault on rationality." Here he critiques the notion of scientific writing as "fictive" (p. 32) (Rowlinson, Hassard, & Decker, 2014); rejection of the "idea that management could be understood on the basis of "positivist factual truth claims" (pp. 32–33) (Novicevic et al., 2014); and opposition to the "dominant science paradigm and its hypothesis-testing methodology" (p. 33) (Decker et al., 2015). Curiously, Bowden selects a quote from Gabrielle Durepos to summarize these problematics:

> As Gabrielle Durepos, arguably the most original of the younger generation of postmodernism (and who declares herself as "amodernist'), has observed, "outright rejection of realism" – understood as "truth claims, objective history, fixed meanings" – is central to postmodernism.
>
> (p. 166)

What is curious about this is that Durepos maintains a strong distinction between postmodernism and amodernism, seeing the production of historical accounts as developed through networks of relations (relationalism) and not as an outcome of relativism. In other words, Durepos identifies herself as a relationalist or amodernist. Hence, the title of the chapter from which this is cited viz. "ANTi-History: Toward Amodern Histories." This error is repeated elsewhere, when Bowden states that "the critical management theorists Gabrielle Durepos and

Albert Mills" claim that Hayden White "was profoundly responsible for "redirecting scholars from a focus on *truth* toward a postmodernist emphasis on the socially constructed nature of the *historical* form" (p. 183). Bowden might have added that Durepos and Mills view the idea of social construction as varied and meaning plural outcomes (i.e., different versions of the same phenomenon) in amodernism and multiple outcomes (i.e., innumerable accounts of phenomena) in postmodernist thinking.

History in translation

Having outlined the various theoretical, ontological, epistemological, methodological and political problems of postmodernism Bowden goes on to warn of its influence in business studies. Here things take a strange turn as Bowden spends time identifying notable postmodernists and sketching their associations. For example, he starts this review of postmodern theorists by stating that "evidence of postmodernist influence within business academia is currently found on many fronts" (p. 201). He names one of those "fronts" as the publication of several special issues of scholarly journals on history and organization,[28] another front is the founding of *Management & Organization History* under the editorship of "the prominent Foucauldian postmodernist Michael Rowlinson" (p. 202). Bowden goes on to also link Rowlinson with *Organization Studies* (where he is a senior editor) and Stephanie Decker "as a frequent co-editor" (p. 202). Decker, in turn, is identified as an Associate Editor of *Business History*. Other cast members include Roy Suddaby – "whose critiques of business "rhetoric" have proved most influential" (p. 202) – is noted as a former Editor and Co-editor the *Academy of Management Review*; Gibson Burrell, "a pioneering advocate of postmodernist perspectives within organizational studies" (p. 202), as a former co-editor of *Organization*[29]; and Stephen Cummings as the incoming co-chair of the Critical Management Studies of the division of the Academy of Management (AoM). Sticking with the AoM, Bowden moves on to the Management History Division to note that he is the current past chair; Dan Wadhwani is the Program Chair; Albert Mills, a "declared *amodernist*" is the Member-at-Large; and Charles Booth is a former Program Chair. Turning to "prominent" books on management and history, Bowden names Bucheli and Wadhwani's (2014) "Organizations in Time"; McLaren, Mills, & Weatherbee's (2015) "Routledge Companion to Management & Organizational History"; Durepos and Mills' (2012) "ANTi-History"; and

Cummings et al.'s (2017) "New History." Much of this part of the exercise ended with a simple listing of notable "supporters of the Historic Turn." This particular vein ends with a simple listing of those who lend supporter to the critical idea of the Historic Turn; linking selected names to their geographical location. This list:

> draws attention to an ever-increasing following that includes, among others[30]: British-based adherents such as John Hassard, Bill Cooke, Peter Clark, Charles Booth, Chris Carter, Alfred Keiser,[31] Scott Taylor, Charles Harvey, Steve Toms, Berard Burnes and Stephanie Decker as well as academics drawn from the United States (Dan Wadhwani, Marcelo Bucheli, Milorad Novicevic, Huseyin Leblebici), Canada (Albert Mills, Patricia McLaren, Terrance Weatherbee, Matthias Kipping, Bill Foster, Austalasia (Stewart Clegg, Stephen Cummings, Todd Bridgeman), and Turkey (Behlül Usdiken).

Finally, Bowden devotes a section of the book to a lengthy critique of Rhetorical History and ANTi-History (see pp. 220–234). Paradoxically, he seems to suggest that Rhetorical History, or the "Rhetorical School,"[32] is the accidental handmaiden of postmodernism. For instance, he writes that, at "first glance, the Rhetoric School appears to owe little to postmodernism," charging that those associated with this focus rarely reference "the term 'postmodernism nor any foundational postmodernist thinkers'" (p. 222). Instead, the problem seems to be guilt by association: "Even where it avoids explicit references to Foucault, White and other like-minded, the work of the Rhetorical School is *subversive* in intent and postmodernist in methodological orientation" (p. 223, our emphasis). Yet, Bowden continues despite [its] pronounced antimodernist sentiments, there remains a strange reluctance in Rhetorical School analysis to explicitly link their formulations to post-modernist theory" (p. 225). Seemingly, in this regard, Rhetorical History is said to share the "unwillingness of advocates of the Historic Turn (Mills and Durepos excepted) to carefully explain the theoretical roots of their intellectual positions" (p. 215). As a result, Bowden continues, this exposes these approaches "to significant, if as yet unacknowledged conceptual, and methodological problems, problems that undermine the credibility of their critiques of modernity" (pp. 215–216).

In apparent contrast, Bowden argues that the theoretical roots of ANTi-History are more transparent, at different points referring to

Gabrielle Durepos (p. 166) and Albert Mills (p. 202) as "declared *amodernist*[s] (p. 202). Yet, as stated in the following quote, this tends to obfuscate rather than clarify:

'Readers of Gabrielle Durepos and Albert Mills' ANTi-History are . . . left in no doubt as to their postmodernist – or to be more exact, *amodernist* – allegiances, with the authors declaring that "ANTi-History draws on Foucault's scholarship. The influence of White, and more particular Latour, is also freely acknowledged" (p. 215, original emphasis).

Once again Bowden draws on ANTi-History to launch an attack on postmodernism, arguing that ANTi-History is "the most significant attempt to address the internal failings of postmodernist thought in management and organizational studies" (p. 231). In particular, Bowden focuses on statements by Durepos that question the postmodern notion that "expectations of the social that reduce everything to text" (p. 231) and "relativism" – "conceding the point that it 'often' produces an *anything goes* attitude, in which no standards exist to govern academic efforts" (p. 233; emphasis in the original Durepos article).

Having set up the growing status of ANTi-History and revealed some of its concerns with postmodernist positions, Bowden finally gets to his critique, arguing that like "a person astride a barbed-wire fence, the attempt by Durepos and Mills to thread an amodernist route between modernism and postmodernism lands them in some uncomfortable positions" (p. 233). These positions include their "stated support for 'empiricism'" yet their view of "knowledge as subjective" (p. 233). As Bowden comments, this "makes understanding of *how* knowledge is socially constructed more important than the knowledge itself" (p. 233). This led Bowden to conclude that accordingly we are still left without any guiding principles for discerning the difference between fact and fiction" that ANTi-History "also effectively rules out the possibility of research leading to generalisable theories or principles" (p. 233).

Bringing up the rear

Shortly after the appearance of WWP in 2018 Jeff Muldoon (2018) and Bernardo Batiz-Lazo (2019) published supportive articles in the *JMH*. Muldoon took on the issue of "facts" versus "social construction," while Batiz-Lazo questioned what was new in "New Histories." Both papers are written largely as book reviews and, as such, contain an overview of "New History." Along the way both draw on Bowden's (2017) book to largely reproduce certain key arguments, noting that the influence of postmodernists has "grown exponentially since 2004"

(Muldoon, 2018, p. 126) and especially so since the publication of new history (Muldoon, 2018, p. 127) that those arguing for a HT

> frequently [use] Foucauldian and postmodernist frameworks without acknowledging their source; that facts are stubborn things that can't be explained away, etc. There also seems to be an added perception that Cummings et al. (2017) view the work of "pioneers" such as Wren is outmoded and unfit for use in 'our times.'
>
> (Muldoon, 2018, p. 127)

This seems somewhat emotionally charged and may be talking about the implications of Cummings et al.'s (2017) work rather than something they have actually said.[33] It is followed by a comment designed to raise further ire from some quarters, namely that Wren and Bedeian have come under a sustained attack from those whose work can be broadly considered to be postmodernist" (Muldoon, 2018, p. 126). Nonetheless, Muldoon characterizes New History as "the most ambitious management history undertaking since Wren and George (virtually) started the field in the early 1970s (Muldoon, 2018, p. 127). Yet he rejects New History as a "failure" as a work of history, faulting it as "polemic" rather than scientific (Muldoon, 2018, p. 127).

Batiz-Lazo (2019) takes an even harsher view of New History, arguing that "the contributors to the 'Historic Turn' still need schooling on the methods to deal with the past" (p. 115); casting doubt on the quality of the earlier work of the New History authors as having not been "subjected to peer review outside the critical management genre" (p. 116); and somehow blaming "the now *infamous* contribution of Clark and Rowlinson (2004)" on the development of the HT (Batiz-Lazo, 2019, p. 115, our emphasis). The last comment is surely an odd one and not designed to help with further debate. Taking aim at the idea of "New" History, Batiz-Lazo characterizes the book as having not added anything new to the debate, calling it a "tedious and repetitive reminder of Foucault's grand method" (p. 117). Finally, in a comment that we, in large part, agree with, Batiz-Lazo contends:

> [If] we are to produce a "new history of management", then we ought to include other neglected constituencies (such as women, LGBTQ+ community, ethnic minorities, different forms of socio-economic racism or management and managerialism in recently-industrialized countries) and topics (such as ethics, the formation of standards, globalization or as the authors suggest, sustainability).
>
> (p. 121)

Where we take offense at this is the fact, explored at length in this book, that the entire debate to date has neglected and ignored feminism, postcolonial studies, race, and de-colonial theory. Nowhere does de-colonial theory, feminism, postcolonial studies, or race appear in either WWP or New History; reference to gender fleetingly appears in the latter,[34] while references to women appear in several places throughout WWP – largely focused on female labour statistics. Bowden (2018) manages to refer to three women who made a contribution to management theory – Beatrice Webb, Mary Parker Follett, and Lillian Gilbreth, while Cummings et al. (2017) refer to Mary Gilson.

Summary: history in translation

Our focus on a particular phenomenon – "the historic turn in management and organization studies" – was used as a heuristic for exploring researchers, debates, events, networks, and selected things (e.g., journals and conferences) involved in a particular area of enquiry – Management and Organizational History. We set out to reveal something about how "history" is produced and the widespread discussions on the relationship between "history and the past" and between history and organization. From our various experiences and research for this book we have gained an impression of a field of enquiry where debate has largely been about the nature of history and the past rather than between history and organization studies. This, we conjecture, is in large part due to the various confusions and opinions about the nature of history that need to be reconciled before, or in the process of, trying to find some form of fusion between history and organization studies. Some (e.g., factual historians) tend to see history as field of enquiry that is quite different from organization students. Others (e.g., postmodernists) tend to see an overlap between history and organization in methodological approach, for example, where understandings of past and present events are open to enquiry though some form of discourse analysis which united the two.

In the meantime, we have tried to reveal the marginalizing effects of the HT, which, more often than not, was overly focused on characterizing history rather than taking into account who benefits from the outcome and to what end.

Until now there has almost been a kind of popular front of those calling for a HT in MOS as they work through the questions: what is history, what is the past, what is the organization, what, if anything, are the relationships between these entities, and who or what gains in the process. But it is clear that when the HT has primarily taken a critical turn (Cummings et al., 2017), it has been perceived as something of a disturbance to mainstream business and management historians, while the largely methodological character of the debate has raised concerns from feminists, postcolonial and de-colonial theorists, and people of colour who are largely shut out of the debate until now.

Notes

1 This section is based on the Special Issue of *M&OH* edited by Mills, Suddaby, Foster, and Durepos (2016) called "Re-visiting the historic turn ten years later."

2 With what veracity and to what extent has yet to be explored. The point being that these communities of practice were largely in the background of the historic turn debates.

3 Mick Rowlinson was the journal's editor at this time.

4 Much of the research draws on feminist historians and organizational analysts, including Joan Acker, Karen Ashcraft, Judith Butler, Natalie Zemon Davies, Barbara Ehrenreich, Kathy Ferguson, Olive Hufton, Luce Irigaray, Julia Kristeva, Joanne Martin, Sheila Rowbotham, and Joan Wallach Scott.

5 Our selection was based on three of the main management and organizational journals based in the UK in 2006. We chose 2006 as a point that coincides with Booth and Rowlinson's (2006) critical call for a historic turn and a point at which *M&OH* was founded and the *JMH* was revived as a journal separate from *Management Decision*. We also selected these three journals because they formed part of the immediate intellectual environment that Phillips and Rippin were writing in. We readily accept that our selection is not representative of other business history journals but that it does provide important insights into the type and form of neglect that Phillips and Rippin were addressing.

6 See also Hearn and Parkin (1983), and Tancred and Mills (1992).

7 Similarly, Russell's (2015) study of "organization men and women and the making of managers" briefly discusses the neglect of Mary Parker Follett's work in the development of management theory. He also goes on to discuss how women's role in developing organizational training programs is neglected in the literature. Russell also goes on to point out that his is a rare study of management in Canada (for more on this issue see Coller, McNally, & Mills, 2015; McLaren & Mills, 2015).

8 It will not have escaped the reader that in this paper Follett is viewed as being a recognized figure in management theory – a great advance from previous neglect of her work returned to the subject of Parker Follett in a co-authored paper with Sonia Adam-Ledunois that compared the respective contributions of Follett and Oliver Sheldon.

9 Their research draws on the feminist and postmodernist work of Marta Calas, Michel Foucault, Betty Friedan, Jeff Hearn, Arlie Hochschild, Keith Jenkins, Rosabeth Moss Kanter, Alun Munslow, Wendy Parkin, Sonja O. Rose, Linda Smircich, Sheila Rowbotham, and Chris Weedon.

10 See also Acker and Van Houten (1974).

11 This is excluding the eight articles that appeared in the 2010 Special Issue.

12 She draws on the work of Bobbie Banerjee, Homi Bhabha, Dipesh Chakrabarty, Leena Chandavarkar, Walter Mignolo, Anshuman Prasad, and others.

13 Included in this comment was not only Booth and Rowlinson (2006) but also two special issues of the *Academy of Management Review (AMR)* 2016 and *M&OH* 2016 (see Wanderley & Barros, 2018, p. 81).

14 Another paper on "Avon and Gender in Brazil" (Moura, 2015) deals with Latin American content but does not utilize or engage with postcolonial or de-colonial theory.

15 A term used by some Critical Management Studies adherents to describe members of their perceived community.

16 Here we are searching for clues and illustrations rather than making some definitive statements about the utilization of postmodern historiography. We want to gain an impression of the extent to which postmodernist historiography has made any discernable impact on management and organizational history.

17 See also Cummings, Bridgman, Hassard, and Rowlinson (2017), who contend that "the increasingly critical approach to memory in organization studies has also given rise to what can be called the deconstruction of corporate, or rhetorical, history. [While] Durepos and Mills (2012a, 2012b) in particular have developed a distinctive approach to understanding how historical narratives are developed from archives that draw on Actor-Network Theory, hence their term ANTi-History, which has increasingly been taken up as an approach for conducting historical research in Organization Studies (e.g., Bruce & Nyland, 2011)," pp. 34–35.

18 Cooke, B., Mills, A. J., & Kelley, E. (Eds.). (2006). Special Issue of *Human Relations* on 'The Cold War and Management', *59*(5).

19 Mills, A. J., Helms Mills, J., Weatherbee, T. G., & Durepos, G. (2012). Theorizing the Past: Critical Engagements, *7*(3).

20 Casey, A., Hansen, P. H., Mills, A. J., & Rowlinson, M. (2014). Narratives and Memory in Organizations.

21 Mills, A. J., Suddaby, R., Foster, W., & Durepos, G. (2016) Re-visiting the Historic Turn 10 Years Later: Current Debates in Management and Organizational History. Special Issue of *Management & Organizational History*.

22 Godfrey, P. C., Hassard, J., O'Connor, E. S., Rowlinson, M., & Ruef, M. (2016). Special Topic Forum. What is Organizational History? Toward a Creative Synthesis of History and Organization Studies, *41*(4).

23 Wadhwani, R. D., Suddaby, R., Mordhorst, M., & Popp, A. (2018). History as Organizing: Uses of the Past in Organization Studies. *Organization Studies, 39*(12).

24 All six strategies are taken from Cummings et al. (2017), page 41, with emphases in the original.

25 Network alert! Albert J. Mills and Jean Helms Mills, co-editors of *QROM*, invited Bradley Bowden to submit a guest editorial to the journal with the proviso that there would also be a rebuttal paper (by Simon Mollan, in press).

26 The Special Issue will be edited by Jean Helms Mills, and it is hoped to have, in addition to four papers broadly favouring Bowden's critique, a further direct rebuttal to Bowden as well as a feminist and a postcolonial paper.

27 Here he cites Durepos and Mills (2012a), p. 131.
28 Here he includes the *AMR* (2016), the *Journal of Organizational Change Management* (2009), and the *Journal of Management* (2010).
29 In fact, Burrell, along with Mike Reed, Marta Calas and Linda Smircich, was a co-founder of the journal but he has not been a co-editor for more than a decade.
30 In the spirit of network analysis, we have included the full list. We leave readers to undertake their own research to assess the actual links between these various scholars.
31 The German board and based scholar will likely be amused to discover that he has moved to the UK!
32 This reference comes complete with further naming of a "grouping" of Canadian-based academics, of whom the school is centered on, namely

> Roy Suddaby, Royston Greenwood, Bill Foster, Matthias Kipping, Diego Coraiola, Alison Minkus, Eldon Wiebe), in addition to those drawn from Britain (Stephanie Decker), Scandinavia (Matts Alvesson, Dan Karreman, Juha-Antti, Arjo Laukia, Jari Ojala), the Netherlands (Roland Kroeze, Sjoerd Keulen), and the United States (Christine Quinn Trank, David Chandler).

33 Muldoon references page 31 of New History but nothing on or around that page bears out the comment.
34 This is surprising given the attention to the Hawthorne Studies and the pioneering feminist work of Joan Acker and Donald Van Houten (1974), which is not referenced in either book.

References

Aaltio, I., Mills, A. J., & Helms Mills, J. C. (2002). Special Issue on "Exploring Gendered Organizational Cultures". *Culture and Organization, 8*(2), 77–79.

Acker, J., & Van Houten, D. R. (1974). Differential Recruitment and Control: The Sex Structuring of Organizations. *Administrative Science Quarterly, 9*(2), 152–163.

Adler, P. S., Forbes, L. C., & Willmott, H. (2006). Critical Management Studies: Premises, Practices, Problems, and Prospects. In J. P. Walsh & A. P. Brief (Eds.), *Annals of the Academy of Management* (Vol. 1, pp. 119–179). New York: Lawrence Erlbaum Associates.

Althusser, L. (1970). *For Marx*. New York: Vintage Books.

Alvesson, M., & Willmott, H. (1992). *Critical Management Studies*. London; Newbury Park, CA: Sage.

Andersen, N. A. (2011). Conceptual History and the Diagnosis of the Present. *Management & Organizational History, 6*(3), 248–267.

Ansell, C. (2009). Mary Parker Follett and Pragmatist Organization. In P. S. Adler (Ed.), *The Oxford Handbook of Sociology and Organization Studies. Classical Foundations* (pp. 464–485). Oxford: Oxford University Press.

Arnberg, K., & Svanlund, J. (2016). Mad Women: Gendered Divisions in the Swedish Advertising Industry, 1930–2012. *Business History, 59*(2), 268–291.

Baird, L. S., Post, J. E., & Mahon, J. F. (1990). *Management. Functions and Responsibilities*. New York: Harper & Row.

Batiz-Lazo, B. (2019). What is New in "A New History of Management"? *Journal of Management History, 25*(1), 114–124.

Beach, D. S. (1985). *Personnel the Management of People at Work* (Fifth ed.). New York: MacMillan Publishing Company.

Bell, E. L., & Nkomo, S. (1992). Re-visioning Women Managers' Lives. In A. J. Mills & P. Tancred (Eds.), *Gendering Organizational Analysis* (pp. 235–247). Newbury Park, CA: Sage.

Bedeian, A. (1986). *Management*. New York: Holt, Rinehardt & Winston.

Benson, S. P. (1978). "The Clerking Sisterhood". Rationalization and the Work Culture of Saleswomen in American Department Stores, 1890–1960. *Radical America, 12*, 41–55.

Bettin, C. and Mills, A. J. (2018) "More than A Feminist: Anti-Historical Reflections on Simone De Beauvoir," *Management & Organizational History*, 13 (1), pp. 65–85

Bettin, C., Mills, A. J., & Helms Mills, J. (2016). "The Halifax School": An Actor-Network Analysis of Critical Management Studies and the Sobey PhD in Management Programme. In C. Grey, I. Huault, V. Perret, & L. Taskin (Eds.), *CMS: Global Voices, Local Accent* (pp. 36–53). London: Routledge.

Bloch, M. (1953). *The Historian's Craft*. Toronto: Random House.

Boje, D. M., Gephart, R. P., Jr., & Thatchenkery, T. J. (Eds.). (1996). *Postmodern Management and Organization Theory*. Thousand Oaks, CA: Sage.

Booth, C., & Rowlinson, M. (2006). Management and Organizational History: Prospects. *Management & Organizational History, 1*(1), 5–30.

Bowden, B. (2016). Editorial and Note on the Writing of Management History. *Journal of Management History, 22*(2), 118–129.

Bowden, B. (2017). Editorial. *Journal of Management History, 23*(3), 218–222.

Bowden, B. (2018). *Work, Wealth, & Postmodernism. The Intellectual Conflict at the Heart of Business Endeavour*. London: Palgrave.

Braverman, H. (1974). *Labor and Monopoly Capital*. New York: Monthly Review Press.

Bristol, D. W., Jr. (2010). The History of Black Business in America: Capitalism, Race, Entrepreneurship, by Juliet E.K. Walker, Chapel Hill, University of North Carolina Press. *Business History, 52*(5), 865–867.

Brown, C. G. (2005). *Postmodernism for Historians*. London: Pearson.

Bruce, K., & Nyland, C. (2011). Elton Mayo and the Deification of Human Relations. *Organization Studies, 32*(3), 383–405. doi:10.1177/0170840610397478

Brunninge, O., & Melander, A. (2016). The Dynamics of Path Dependence on the Individual, Organizational and Fields Levels: MoDo, the Kempe Family and the Swedish Pulp and Paper Industry 1873–1990. *Management & Organizational History, 11*(2), 189–210.

Bryman, A., Bell, E., Mills, A. J., & Yue, A. R. (2011). *Business Research Methods. First Canadian Edition*. Toronto: Oxford University Press.

Bucheli, M., & Wadhwani, D. (Eds.). (2014). *Organizations in Time. History, Theory, Methods*. Oxford: Oxford University Press.

Burrell, G. (1984). Sex and Organizational Analysis. *Organization Studies, 5*(2), 97–118.

Burrell, G. (1987). No Accounting for Sexuality. *Accounting, Organizations, and Society, 12*, 89–101.

Burrell, G. (1988). Modernism, Postmodernism and Organizational Analysis 2: The contribution of Michel Foucault. *Organisation Studies, 9*, 221–235.

Burrell, G. (1997). *Pandemonium: Towards a Retro-organization Theory*. London: Sage.

Burrell, G. (1998). The Contribution of Michel Foucault. In A. McKinlay & K. Starkey (Eds.), *Foucault, Management and Organization Theory* (pp. 124–138). London: Sage.

Burrell, G., & Morgan, G. (1979). *Sociological Paradigms and Organizational Analysis*. London: Heinemann.

Burrell, G., Reed, M. I., Calás, M. B., Smircich, L., & Alvesson, M. (1994). Why Organization? Why Now? *Organization, 1*(1), 5–17. doi:10.1177/1350508 49400100101

Burton, A. (2005a). Introduction, Archive Fever, Archive Stories. In A. Burton (Ed.), *Archive Stories: Facts, Fictions, and the Writing of Histroy* (pp. 1–24). London: Duke University Press.

Burton, A. (Ed.). (2005b). *Archive Stories. Fact, Fictions, and The Writing of History.* Durham, NC: Duke University.

Calás, M. B. (1992). An/Other Silent Voice? Representing "Hispanic Woman" in Organizational Texts. In A. J. Mills & P. Tancred (Eds.), *Gendering Organizational Analysis* (pp. 201–221). London: Sage.

Calás, M. B., & Smircich, L. (1992). Re-writing Gender into Organizational Theorizing: Directions from Feminist Perspectives. In M. Reed & M. Hughes (Eds.), *Rethinking Organization: New Directions in Organizational Theory and Analysis* (pp. 227–254). London: Sage.

Calás, M. B., & Smircich, L. (1996). Not Ahead of Her Time: Reflections on Mary Parker Follett as Prophet of Management. *Organization, 3*(1), 147–152. doi:10.1177/135050849631008

Calás, M. B., & Smircich, L. (Eds.). (1997). *Postmodern Management Theory.* Aldershot: Ashgate.

Calás, M. B., & Smircich, L. (2005). From the 'Woman's Point of View' Ten Years Later: Towards a Feminist Organization Studies In S. Clegg, C. Hardy, T. Lawrence, & W. Nord (Eds.), *The Sage Handbook of Organization Studies* (pp. 284–346). London: Sage.

Calás, M. B., Smircich, L., & Holvino, E. (2014). Theorizing Gender-and-Organization: Changing Times … Changing Theories? In S. Kumra, R. Simpson, & R. J. Burke (Eds.), *The Oxford Handbook of Gender and Organizations* (pp. 17–52). Oxford: University Press.

Callon, M. (1986). Some Elements of a Sociology of Translation: Domestification of the Scallops and the Fisherman of St Brieuc Bay. In J. Law (Ed.), *Power, Action and Belief: A New Sociology of Knowledge?* (Vol. Sociological Review Monograph 32; pp. 196–233). London: Routledge & Kegan Paul.

Callon, M., & Latour, B. (1981). Unscrewing the Big Leviathan: How Actors Macro-structure Reality and How Sociologists Help Them to Do So. In K. Knorr-Cetina & A. V. Cicourel (Eds.), *Advances in Social Theory and Methodology: Towards an Integration of Micro and Macro-sociologies* (pp. 227–303). Boston: Routledge & Kegan Paul.

Carr, D. (1986). *Time, Narrative, and History.* Bloomingdale, IL; Indianapolis: Indiana University Press.

Carson, K. D., Carson, P. P., & Phillips, J. S. (1997). *The ABCs of Collaborative Change: The Manager's Guide to Library Renewal.* Chicago, IL: American Library Association.

Carter, C., McKinlay, A., & Rowlinson, M. (2002). Introduction: Foucault, Management and History. *Organization, 9*(4), 515–526.

Cifor, M., & Wood, S. (2017). Critical Feminism in the Archives. In M. Caswell, R. Punzalan, & T.-K. Sangwand (Eds.), *Critical Archival Studies. Special Issue of the Journal of Critical Library and Information Studies* (Vol. 2, pp. 1–27). Litwin Books, Sacramento, CA.

Clark, P., & Blundel, R. (2007); Penrose, Critical Realism and the Evolution of Business Knowledge: A Methodological Re-appraisal. *Management & Organizational History, 2*(1), 45–62.

Clark, P., & Rowlinson, M. (2004). The Treatment of History in Organization Studies: Toward an "Historic Turn"? *Business History, 46*(3), 331–352.

Clegg, S. R. (1981). Organization and Control. *Administrative Sciences Quarterly, 26,* 532–545.

Clegg, S. R. (1989). *Frameworks of Power.* Newbury Park, CA: Sage.

Clegg, S. R., & Dunkerley, D. (1977). *Critical Issues in Organizations.* London; Boston, MA: Routledge & Kegan Paul.

Clegg, S. R., & Dunkerley, D. (1980). *Organization, Class and Control.* London: Routledge & Kegan Paul.

Clegg, S. R., Ibarra Colado, E., & Bueno-Rodriques, L. (1999). *Global Management: Universal Theories and Local Realities.* London; Thousand Oaks, CA: Sage Publications.

Coller, K. E., Helms Mills, J., & Mills, A. J. (2016). The British Airways Heritage Collection: An Ethnographic 'History'. *Business History, 58*(4), 547–570.

Coller, K. E., McNally, C., & Mills, A. J. (2015). The Inner Circle: Towards a 'Canadian' Management History – Key Canadian Contributors to New Institution Theory. In P. G. McLaren, A. J. Mills, & T. G. Weatherbee (Eds.), *The Routledge Companion to Management and Organizational History* (pp. 342–360). London: Routledge.

Cooke, B. (1999). Writing the Left Out of Management Theory: The Historiography of the Management of Change. *Organization, 6*(1), 81–105.

Cooke, B. (2003a). The Denial of Slavery in Management Studies. *Journal of Management Studies 40,* 1895–1918.

Cooke, B. (2003b). Managing Organizational Culture and Imperialism. In A. Pradas (Ed.), *Postcolonial Theory and Organizational Analysis: A Critical Engagement* (pp. 75–94). London: Palgrave.

Cooke, B. (2004). The Managing of the (Third) World. *Organization, 11*(5), 603–629. doi:10.1177/1350508404044063

Cooke, B. (2009). The Tavistock's Everyday Use of Benzedrine, and More: On the Multipe Significances of DB, Scholar-Publisher. *Management & Organizational History, 4*(2), 203–206.

Cooper, R., & Burrell, G. (1988). Modernism, Postmodernism and Organizational Analysis: An Introduction. *Organization Studies, 9*(1), 91–112.

Corbett, J. M. (2008). Towards Neuroscientific Management? Geometric Chronophotography and the Thin Slicing of the Labouring Body. *Management & Organizational History, 3*(2), 107–125.

Corman, S. R., & Poole, M. S. (2000). *Perspectives on Organizational Communication: Finding Common Ground.* New York: Guilford Press.

Corrigan, L. T. (2015). *Budget Theatre: A Postdramaturgical Account of Municipal Budget Making* (PhD). Saint Mary's, Halifax, Nova Scotia.

Corrigan, L. T. (2016). Accounting Practice and the Historic Turn: Performing Budget Histories. *Management & Organizational History*, 1–22. doi:10.1080/17449359.2015.1115743

Corrigan, L. T., & Mills, A. J. (2012). Men on Board: Can Actor-Network Theory Critique the Persistence of Gender Inequity? *Management & Organizational History, 7*(3), 251–265.

Costea, B., Crump, N., & Holm, J. (2006). Conceptual History and the Interpretation of Managerial Ideologies. *Management & Organizational History, 1*(2), 159–176.

Crowley, M. J. (2016). 'Inequality' and 'Value' Reconsidered? The Employment of Post Office Women, 1910–1922. *Business History, 58*(7), 985–1007.

Crump, N., Ameridis, K., & Costea, B. (2007). A Historical-Cultural Approach to the Study of Business Ethics Using the Modern Novel: An Illustration. *Management & Organizational History, 2*(3), 237–254.

Cummings, S., Bridgman, T., Hassard, J., & Rowlinson, M. (2017). *A New History of Managment*. Cambridge: Cambridge University Press.

Daley, R. (1980). *An American Saga. Juan Trippe and His Pan Am Empire*. New York: Random House.

Damart, S. (2013). How Mary P. Follett's Ideas on Management Have Emerged: An Analysis Based on Her Practical Management Experience and Her Political Philosophy. *Journal of Management History, 19*(4), 459–473. doi:10.1108/JMH-05-2012-0041

Davis, K., & Newstrom, J. W. (1985). *Human Behavior at Work: Organizational Behavior* (Seventh ed.). New York: McGraw-Hill.

Davis, N. Z. (1983). *The Return of Martin Guerre*. Cambridge, MA: Harvard University Press.

Deal, Nick, Mills, Albert. J. and Helms Mills, Jean. (2019) 'Amodern and modern warfare in the making of a commercial airline.' *Management and Organizational History*, 13 (4), pp. 373–396.

Decker, S. (2013). The Silence of the Archives: Business History, Postcolonialism and Archival Ethnography. *Management & Organizational History, 8*(2), 155–173.

Decker, S. (2016). Paradigms Lost: Integrating History and Organization Studies. *Management & Organizational History, 11*(4), 364–379.

Decker, S., Kipping, M., & Wadhwani, R. D. (2015). New Business Histories! Plurality in Business History Research Methods. *Business History, 57*(1), 30–40.

Derrida, J. (1995). *Archve Fever: A Freudian Impression*. Chicago, IL: University of Chicago Press.

Donaldson, L. (1985). *In Defence of Organization Theory*. Cambridge: Cambridge University Press.

Durepos, G. (2015). ANTi-History: Toward Amodern Histories. In P. G. McLaren, A. J. Mills, & T. G. Weatherbee (Eds.), *The Routledge Companion to Management and Organizational History* (pp. 153–180). London: Routledge.

Durepos, G., McKinlay, A., & Taylor, S. (2017). Narrating Histories of Women at Work: Archives, Stories, and the Promise of Feminism. *Business History, 59*(8), 1–19.

Durepos, G., & Mills, A. J. (2012a). Actor Network Theory, ANTi-History, and Critical Organizational Historiography. *Organization, 19*(6), 703–721.

Durepos, G., & Mills, A. J. (2012b). *ANTi-History: Theorizing the Past, History, and Historiography in Management and Organizational Studies*. Charlotte, NC: Information Age Publishing.

Durepos, G., & Mills, A. J. (2018). ANTi-History: An Alternative Approach to History. In C. Cassell, A. L. Cunliffe, & G. Grandy (Eds.), *The SAGE Handbook of Qualitative Business and Management Research Methods* (pp. 431–449). London: Sage.

Durepos, G., Mills, A. J., & Helms Mills, J. (2008). Tales in the Manufacture of Knowledge: Writing a Company History of Pan American World Airways. *Management & Organizational History, 3*(1), 63–80.

Durepos, G., Mills, A. J., & Weatherbee, T. G. (2012). Theorizing the Past: Realism, Relativism, Relationalism and the Reassembly of Weber. *Management & Organizational History, 7*(3), 267–281.

Ellis, R., & McCutcheon, J. (1996). Tracing the Development of a Business School Through Oral History. *Proceeding of the 1995 Administrative Sciences Association of Canada, Business History Division, 16*, 64–69.

Elton, G. R. (2002). *The Practice of History* (Second ed.). Oxford: Blackwell.

Eriksson, L. (2014). Beneficiaries or Policyholders? The Role of Women in Swedish Life Insurance 1900–1950. *Business History, 56*(8), 1335–1360.

Ermarth, E. D. (1992). *Sequel to History: Postmodernism and the Crisis of Representational Time*. Princeton, NJ: Princeton University Press.

Faria, A., Ibarra-Colado, E., & Guedes, A. (2010). Internationalization of Management, Neoliberalism and the Latin America Challenge. *Critical Perspectives on International Business, 6*(2/3), 97–115. doi:10.1108/17422041011049932

Flynn, J. R. (1996). Group differences: Is good society possible? *Journal of Biosocial Science, 28*(4), 673–585.

Foster, J., Mills, A. J., & Weatherbee, T. G. (2014). History, Field Definition and Management Studies: The Case of the New Deal. *Journal of Management History, 20*(2), 179–199.

Foster, W. M., Coraiola, D. M., Suddaby, R., Kroezen, J., & Chandler, D. (2017). The Strategic Use of Historical Narratives: A Theoretical Framework. *Business History, 59*(8), 1176–1200.

Foster, W. M., Suddaby, R., Minkus, A., & Wiebe, E. (2011). History as Social Memory Assets: The Example of Tim Hortons. *Management & Organizational History, 6*(1), 101–120.

Foucault, M. (1970). *The Order of Things: An Archaeology of the Human Sciences*. London: Routledge.

Foucault, M. (1972). *The Archaeology of Knowledge*. London: Routledge.

Foucault, M. (1980). *Power/knowledge: Selected Interviews and Other Writings 1972- 1977*. Gordon, C. (ed.). 1st ed., New York, Pantheon Books.

Fox-Genovese, E. (1982). Placing Women's History in History. *New Left Review, 1*(133), 5–29.

Fritzsche, P. (2005). The Archive and the Case of the German Nation. In A. Burton (Ed.), *Archive Strories* (pp. 184–208). Durham, NC: Duke University Press.

Frost, P. J. (1994). Crossroads. *Organization Science, 5*(4), 608–620.

Furtado, P. (Ed.). (2018). *Histories of Nations: How their Identities were Forged.* London: Thames & Hudson.

Gadamer, H. G. (1976). *Philosophical Hermeneutics*: Berkeley: Univerisity of California Press.

Garfinkel, H. (1967). *Studies in Ethnomethodology.* Englewood Cliffs, NJ: Prentice Hall.

George, C. S. (1968). *The History of Management Thought.* Englewood Cliffs, NJ: Prentice-Hall, Inc.

George, C. S. (1972). *The History of Management Thought* (Second ed.). Englewood Cliffs, NJ: Prentice-Hall.

Ghosh, D. (2005). National Narratives and the Politics of Miscegenation. In A. Burton (Ed.), *Archive Stories. Facts, Fictions, and the Writing of History* (pp. 27–44). Durham, NC: Duke University Press.

Ginzburg, C. (1976). *The Cheese and the Worms.* London: Routlege & Kegan Paul.

Gosh, D. (2005). National Narratives and the Politics of Miscegenation. In A. Burton (Ed.), *Archive Stories: Facts, Fictions, and the Writing of History* (pp. 27–44). London: Duke University Press.

Graham, P. (1996). *Mary Parker Follett: Prophet of Management.* Cambridge, MA: Harvard Business School Press.

Gramsci, A. (1978). *The Modern Prince and Other Writings.* New York: International Publishers.

Grant, J. D., & Mills, A. J. (2006). The Quiet Americans: Formative Context, the Academy of Management Leadership, and the Management textbook, 1936–1960. *Management & Organizational History, 1*(2), 201–224.

Greenwood, A., & Bernardi, A. (2014). Understanding the Rift, the (Still) Uneasy Bedfellows of History and Organization Studies. *Organization, 21*(6), 907–932. doi:10.1177/1350508413514286

Gundersen, Y. R. (2003). On the Dark Side of History. Retrieved from www.eurozine.com/on-the-dark-side-of-history/

Gutek, B. A. (1985). *Sex and the Workplace.* San Francisco, CA: Jossey-Bass.

Haggerty, S. (2010). Book Review: Enterprising Women and Shipping in the Nineteenth Century, by Helen Doe, Woodbridge, Boydell Press, ISBN 978-1-84383-472-4. *Business History, 52*(2), 342.

Hannam, J. (2010). The Victory of Ideals Must be Organized: Labour Party Women Organizers in the Inter-war Years. *Management & Organizational History, 5*(3–4), 331–348.

Hartt, C. M. (2013). Actants Without Actors: Polydimensional Discussion of a Regional Conference. *Tamara: Journal for Critical Organization Inquiry, 11*(3), 15–25.

Hartt, C. M., Helms Mills, J., & Mills, A. J. (2012). Reading between the Lines: Gender, Work, and History: The Case of the Nova Scotia Teachers' Union. *Journal of Management History, 18*(1), 82–95.

Hartt, C. M., Mills, A. J., Helms Mills, J, & Corrigan, L. T. (2014). Sense-making and Actor Networks: The Non-corporeal Actant and the Making of an Air Canada History. *Management & Organizational History, 9*(3), 288–304. doi:10.1080/17449359.2014.920260

Hartt, C. M., Mills, A. J., Helms Mills, J., & Durepos, G. (2012). Markets, Organizations, Institutions and National Identity: Pan American Airways, Postcoloniality and Latin America. *Critical Perspectives on International Business, 8*(1), 14–36.

Hassard, J. (1991). Multiple Paradigms and Organizational Analysis: A Case Study. *Organization Studies, 12*(2), 275–299. doi:10.1177/017084069101200206

Hassard, J. (2012). Rethinking the Hawthorne Studies: The Western Electric Research in Its Social, Political and Historical Context. *Human Relations, 65*(11), 1431–1461. doi:10.1177/0018726712452168

Hassard, J., Hogan, J., & Rowlinson, M. (2001). From Labor Process Theory to Critical Management Studies. *Administative Theory & Praxis, 23*(3), 339–362.

Hassard, J., & Wolfram Cox, J. (2013). Can Sociological Paradigms Still Inform Organizational Analysis? A Paradigm Model for Post-paradigm Times. *Organization Studies, 34*(11), 1701–1728. doi:10.1177/0170840613495019

Hearn, J., & Parkin, P. W. (1983). Gender and Organizations: A Selective Review and a Critique of a Neglected Area. *Organization Studies, 4*(3), 219–242.

Hearn, J., Sheppard, D., Tancred-Sheriff, P., & Burrell, G. (Eds.). (1989). *The Sexuality of Organization.* London: Sage.

Hearn, J., Lamsa, A.-M., Biese, I., Heikkinen, S., Louvrier, J., Niemisto, C., & Hirvonen, P. (2015). *Opening Up New Opportunities in Gender Equality Work.* Helsinki: Hanken School of Economics.

Hiltzik, M. (2011). *The New Deal. A Modern History.* New York: Free Press.

Hobsbawn, E. (1997). *On history,* New Press: NY.

Holden, K. (2010). Other People's Children: Single Women and Residential Childcare in Mid-20th Century England. *Management & Organizational History, 5*(3–4), 314–330.

Honeyman, K. (2010). Book Review: The Foundations of Female Entrepreneurship. Enterprise, Home and Household in London, c.1800–1870, by Alison C. Kay, London, Routledge, 2009. *Business History, 52*(2), 340–342.

Hopfl, H. (2010). The Death of the Heroine. *Management & Organizational History, 5*(3–4), 395–407.

Humphreys, J. H., Novicevic, M. M., Hayek, M., Gibson, J. W., Pane Haden, S. S., & Williams, W. A. (2016). Disharmony in New Harmony: Insights from the Narcissistic Leadership of Robert Owen. *Journal of Management History, 22*(2), 146–170.

Hunter, S. & Swan, E. (2007). Oscillating politics and shifting agencies: equalities and diversity work and actor network theory, *Equal Opportunities International*, Vol. 26 Issue: 5, pp. 402–419.

Ibarra-Colado, E. (2006). Organization Studies and Epistemic Coloniality in Latin America: Thinking Otherness from the Margins. *Organization*, *13*(4), 463–488.

Ibarra-Colado, E., Faria, A., & Lucia Guedes, A. (2010). Introduction to the Special Issue on "Critical International Management and International Critical Management: Perspectives from Latin America". *Critical Perspectives on International Business, 6*(2/3), 86–96. doi:10.1108/17422041011049923

Iggers, G. (1997). *Historiography in the Twentieth Century: From Scientific Objectivity to the Postmodern Challenge*. Hanover, NH: Wesleyan University Press.

Jacques, R. (1996). *Manufacturing the Employee: Management Knowledge from the 19th to 21st Centuries*. London: Sage.

Jammulamadaka, N. (2016). Bombay Textile Mills: Exploring CSR Roots in Colonial India. *Journal of Management History, 22*(4), 450–472.

Jarvis, P. (2014). *British Airways. An Illustrated History*. Gloucestershire: Amberley.

Jenkins, K. (1991). *Re-thinking history*. London; New York: Routledge.

Jenkins, K. (1995). *On 'What is History?': From Carr and Elton to Rorty and White*. London: Routledge.

Johnson, P., & Duberley, J. (2000). *Understanding Management Research*. London: Sage.

Jones, N., Novicevic, M. M., Hayek, M., & Humphreys, J. H. (2012). The First Documents of Emancipated African American Management. *Journal of Management History, 18*(1), 46–60.

Josephson, M. (1943). *Empire of the Air, Juan Trippe and the Struggle for World Airways*. New York: Harcourt Brace and Co.

Josephson, M. (1944). *Empire of the Air*. New York: Harcourt, Brace and Company.

Joullié, J.-E. (2018). Management Without Theory for the Twenty-First Century. *Journal of Management History, 24*(4), 377–395.

Kalela, J. (2012). *Making History. The Historian and Uses of the Past*. London: Palgrave MacMillan.

Kanter, R. M. (1977). *Men and Women of the Corporation*. New York: Basic Books.

Kerr, R., Robinson, S. K., & Elliott, C. (2016). Modernism, Postmodernism, and Corporate Power: Historicizing the Architectural Typology of the Corporate Campus. *Management & Organizational History, 11*(2), 123–146.

Kieser, A. (1994). Why Organizational Theory Needs Historical Analyses – And How This Should be Performed. *Organization Science, 5*(4), 608–620.

Kieser, A. (1997). Rhetoric and Myth in Management Fashion. *Organization, 4*(1), 49–74.

Kieser, A. (2004). The Americanization of Academic Management Education in Germany. *Journal of Management Inquiry, 13*(2), 90–98.

Kieser, A. (2015). Twenty Years After. Why Organization Theory Needs Historical Analysis. In P. G. McLaren, A. J. Mills, & T. G. Weatherbee (Eds.), *The Routledge Companion to Management and Organizational History* (pp. 47–48). London: Routlede.

Koontz, H. D. (1961). The Management Theory Jungle. *Journal of the Academy of Management, 4*(3), 174–188.

Krenn, M. (2011). From Scientific Management to Homemaking: Lillian M. Gilbreth's Contributions to the Development of Management Thought. *Management & Organizational History, 6*(2), 145–161.

Kroeze, R., & Keulen, S. (2013). Leading a Multinational is History in Practice: The Use of Invented Traditions and Narratives at AkzoNobel, Shell, Philips and ABN AMRO. *Business History, 55*(8), 1265–1287.

Kuhn, A., & Wolpe, A. (1978). *Feminism and Materialism: Women and Modes of Production.* London: Routledge & Kegan Paul Ltd.

Kuhn, T. S. (1962). *The Structure of Scientific Revolutions.* Chicago, IL: University of Chicago Press.

Kuokkanen, A., & Seeck, H. (2013). Subtle Resistance to Normative Management Ideas in a Masculine-gendered Corporate Culture. *Management & Organizational History, 8*(3), 214–230.

Lamond, D. (2005). On the Value of Management History. Absorbing the Past to Understand the Present and Inform the Future. *Management Decision, 43*(10), 1273–1281.

Latour, B. (1993). *We Have Never Been Modern.* Cambridge, MA: Harvard University Press.

Latour, B. (2005). *Reassembling the Social: An Introduction to Actor-Network-Theory.* Oxford: Oxford University Press.

Latour, B., & Woolgar, S. (1979). *Laboratory Life: The Social Construction of Scientific Facts.* Beverly Hills, CA: Sage Publications.

Leblebici, H., & Shah, N. (2004). The Birth, Transformation and Regeneration of Business Incubators as New Organisational Forms: Understanding the Interplay between Organisational History and Organisational Theory. *Business History, 46*(3), 353–380.

Lemisch, J. (1975). *On Active Service in War and Peace. Politics and Ideology in the American Historical Profession.* Toronto: New Hogtown Press.

Lerner, Gerda. (1986). *The Creation of Patriarchy.* New York: Oxford University Press.

L'Estrange, S. (2014). Historical Research. In J. Mills & M. Birks (Eds.), *Qualitative Methodology. A Practical Guide.* (pp. 123–144) Thousand Oaks, CA: Sage.

Lubinski, C. (2018). From 'History as Told' to 'History as Experienced': Contextualizing the Uses of the Past. *Organization Studies, 39*(12), 1785–1809.

Lyke, A. (2017). Habitus, Doxa, and Saga: Applications of Bourdieu's Theory of Practice to Organizational History. *Management & Organizational History, 12*(2), 163–173.

Lyotard, J.-F. (1979). *La condition postmoderne: rapport sur le savoir.* Paris: Éditions de Minuit.

Maclean, M., Harvey, C., & Clegg, S. R. (2015). Conceptualizing Historical Organization Studies. *Academy of Management Review, 41*(4), 609–632.

Maclean, M., Harvey, C., Sillince, J. A. A., & Golant, B. D. (2014). Living Up to the Past? Ideological Sensemaking in Organizational Transition. *Organization, 21*(4), 543–567.

Magnússon, S. G., & Szijártó, I. M. (2013). *What is Microhistory? Theory and Practice.* London: Routledge.

Maielli, G. (2007). Counterfactuals, Superfactuals, and the Problematic Relationship between Business Management and the Past. *Management & Organizational History, 2*(4), 275–294.

Marcuse, H. (1964). *One-Dimensional Man: Studies in the Ideology of Advanced Industrial Society.* New York: Beacon Press.

Marshall, D. R., & Novicevic, M. M. (2016). Legitimizing the Social Enterprise: Development of a Conformance Framework Based on a Genealogical Pragmatic Analysis. *Management & Organizational History, 1–24.* doi:10.1080/17449359.2016.1151362

Marx, K. (1844/1967). *Economic and Philosophic Manuscripts of 1844.* Moscow: Progress Publishers.

Marx, K. (1999). *Capital: A Critical Analysis of Capitalist Production* (Abridged ed.). London: Oxford University Press.

Mayo, E. (1933). *The Human Problems of an Industrial Civilization.* New York: MacMillan.

McCann, L. (2016). 'Management is the Gate' – But to Where? Rethinking Robert McNamara's 'Career Lessons'. *Management & Organizational History, 11*(2), 166–188.

McCloskey, D. (1994). *Knowledge and Persuasion in Economics.* Cambridge: Cambridge University Press.

McDonald, T. J. (1996). Introduction. In T. J. Morgan (Ed.), *The Historic Turn in the Human Sciences* (pp. 1–2). Ann Arbor: University of Michigan Press.

McKinlay, A. (2006). Managing Foucault: Genealogies of Management. *Management & Organizational History, 1*(1), 87–100.

McKinlay, A. (2013). Following Foucault into the Archives: Clerks, Careers and Cartoons. *Management & Organizational History, 8*(2), 137–154. doi:10.1080/17449359.2012.761498

McLaren, P. G., & Mills, A. J. (2015). History and the Absence of Canadian Management Theory. In P. G. McLaren, A. J. Mills, & T. G. Weatherby (Eds.), *Routledge Companion to Management & Organizational History* (pp. 319–331). London: Routledge.

Mignolo, W. D. (1991). *The Idea of Latin America.* Oxford: Blackwell.

Mignolo, W. D. (2007). Delinking: The Rhetoric of Modernity, the Logic of Coloniality and the Grammar of De-coloniality. *Cultural Studies, 21*(2–3), 449–514.

Mills, A. J. (1988). Gareth Morgan: An Interview. *Aurora, 11*(2), 42–46.

Mills, Albert J., & Tancred, Peta (Eds.). (1992). *Gendering organizational analysis*. Newbury Park: Sage Publications.

Mills, A. J. (1995). Man/Aging Subjectivity, Silencing Diversity: Organizational Imagery in the Airline Industry – The Case of British Airways. *Organization, 2*(2), 243–269.

Mills, A. J. (1997). Duelling Discourses – Desexualization Versus Eroticism in the Corporate Framing of Female Sexuality in the British Airline Industry, 1945–60. In P. Prasad, A. J. Mills, M. Elmes, & A. Prasad (Eds.), *Managing the Organizational Melting Pot: Dilemmas of Workplace Diversity* (pp. 171–198). Newbury Park, CA: Sage.

Mills, A. J. (2002). Studying the Gendering of Organisational Culture over Time: Concerns Issues and Strategies. *Gender Work and Organisation, 9*(3), 286–307.

Mills, A. J. (2006). *Sex, Strategy and the Stratosphere: Airlines and the Gendering of Organizational Culture*. London: Palgrave Macmillan.

Mills, A. J. (Ed.). (2017). *Insights and Research on the Study of Gender and Intersectionality in International Airline Cultures*. Bradford: Emerald Books.

Mills, A. (2017). *The Gendering of Organizational Culture: Social and Organizational Discourses in the Making of British Airways, Insights and Research on the Study of Gender and Intersectionality in International Airline Cultures*, Emerald Publishing Limited, Bingley, UK.

Mills, A. J., & Helms Mills, J. (2011). Digging Archeology: Postpositivist Theory and Archival Research in Case Study Development. In R. Piekkari & C. Welch (Eds.), *Rethinking the Case Study in International Business Research* (pp. 342–360). Northampton, MA: Edward Elgar Publishing.

Mills, A. J., & Helms Mills, J. (2013). CMS: A Satirical Critique of Three Narrative Histories. *Organization, 20*(1), 117–129.

Mills, A. J., & Helms Mills, J. (2017). Digging Archeology: Postpositivist Theory and Archival Research in Case Study Development. In A. J. Mills (Ed.), *Insights and Research on the Study of Gender and Intersectionality in International Airline Culture*. Bradford: Emerald Books.

Mills, A. J., & Helms Mills, J. (2018). Archival Research. In C. Cassell, A. L. Cunliffe, & G. Grandy (Eds.), *The SAGE Handbook of Qualitative Business and Management Research Methods* (pp. 32–46). London: Sage.

Mills, A. J., Helms Mills, J., Bratton, J., & Foreshaw, C. (2007). *Organizational Behaviour in a Global Context*. Peterborough: Broadview Press.

Mills, A. J., Suddaby, R., Foster, W. M., & Durepos, G. (2016). Re-visiting the Historic Turn 10 Years Later: Current Debates in Management and Organizational History – An Introduction. *Management & Organizational History, 11*(2), 67–76.

Mills, A. J., Weatherbee, T. G., Foster, J., & Helms Mills, J. (2015). The New Deal, History, and Management & Organization studies: Lessons, Insights and Reflections. In P. G. McLaren, A. J. Mills, & T. G. Weatherbee (Eds.), *Routledge Companion to Management & Organizational History* (pp. 265–284). London: Routledge.

Mills, C. W. (1959). *The Sociological Imagination*. London: Oxford University Press.

Miskell, P. (2018). Reflections on the Integration of History and Organization Studies. *Management & Organizational History, 13*(3), 213–219.

Mollan, S. (2019) Phenomenal differences: varieties of historical interpretation in management and organization studies. *Qualitative Research in Organizations and Management* (in press)

Moore, N., Salter, A., Stanley, L., & Tamboukou, M. (Eds.). (2017). *The Archive Project: Archival Research in the Social Sciences*. London: Routledge.

Mordhorst, M. (2008). From Counter Factual History to Counter-Narrative History. *Management & Organizational History, 3*(1), 5–26.

Mordhorst, M. (2014). Arla and Danish National Identity – Business History as Cultural History. *Business History, 56*(1), 116–133.

Mordhorst, M., & Schwarzkopf, S. (2017). Theorising Narrative in Business History. *Business History, 59*(8), 1155–1175.

Moura, S. (2015). Try It at Home: Avon and Gender in Brazil, 1958–1975. *Business History, 57*(6), 800–821.

Muhr, S. L., & Salem, A. (2013). Specters of Colonialism – Illusionary Equality and the Forgetting of History in a Swedish Organization. *Management & Organizational History, 8*(1), 62–76.

Muldoon, J. (2018). Stubborn Things: Evidence, Postmodernism and the Craft of History. *Journal of Management History.* doi:10.1108/jmh-09–2018–0046

Munslow, A. (2010). *The Future of History*. London: Palgrave MacMillan.

Munslow, A. (2015). Managing the Past. In P. G. McLaren, A. J. Mills, & T. G. Weatherbee (Eds.), *The Routedge Companion to Management and Organizational History* (pp. 129–142). London: Routledge.

Murillo, B. (2009). Book Review of 'Chocolate, Women and Empire: A Social and Cultural History', by Emma Robertson, Manchester, Manchester University Press, 2009. *Business History, 53*(3), 470–472.

Myrick, K., Helms Mills, J., & Mills, A. J. (2012). Actor Network Theory, Historiography, and the Early History of the Academy of Management (1936-195). *Proceedings of the Administrative Sciences Association of Canada, Annual Meeting*, St. John's, Newfoundland, CA, June.

Myrick, K., Helms Mills, J., & Mills, A. J. (2013). History-making and the Academy of Management: An ANTi-History perspective. *Management & Organizational History, 8*(4), 345–370. doi:10.1080/17449359.2013.821662

Nkomo, S. (1992). The Emperor Has No Clothes: Rewriting "Race in Organizations". *Academy of Management Review, 17*(3), 487–513.

Nolte, H.-H. (2010). Book Review: Female Entrepreneurs in Nineteenth-Century Russia, by Galina Ulianova (Translated by Anna and Aleksey Yurasovsky), London, Pickering & Chatto, 2009. *Business History, 52*(2), 678–679.

Nordlund Edvinsson, T. (2015). Standing in the Shadow of the Corporation: Women's Contribution to Swedish Family Business in the Early Twentieth Century. *Business History, 58*(4), 532–546.

Novicevic, M. M, Harvey, M., Buckley, R. M., Wren, D., & Pena, L. (2007). Communities of Creative Practice: Follett's Seminal Conceptualization. *International Journal o0f Public Administration, 30(2)*, 367–385.

Novicevic, M. M., Humphreys, J., Ronald Buckley, M., Roberts, F., Hebdon, A., & Kim, J. (2013). Teaching as Constructive-Developmental Leadership: Insights from Mary Follett. *Journal of Management History, 19*(4), 423–440. doi:10.1108/JMH-09-2012-0060

Novicevic, M. M., Jones, J. L., & Carraher, S. (2015). Decentering Wren's Evolution of Management Thought. In P. G. McLaren, A. J. Mills, & T. G. Weatherbee (Eds.), *The Routledge Companion to Management and Organizational History* (pp. 11–30). London: Routledge.

Novicevic, M. M, Marshall, D. R., Humphreys, J. H., & Seifried, C. (2019). Both Loved and Despised: Uncovering a Process of Collective Contestation in Leadership Identification. *Organization, 20(2)*, 236–254.

Nyland, C., & Heenan, T. (2005). Mary van Kleeck, Taylorism and the Control of Management Knowledge. *Management Decision, 43*(10), 1358–1374.

Nyland, C., & Rix, M. (2000). Mary van Kleeck, Lillian Gilbreth and the Women's Bureau Study of Gendered Labor Law. *Journal of Management History, 6*(7), 306–322.

Oyler, J. D., & Golden Pryor, M. (2009). Workplace Diversity in the United States: The Perspective of Peter Drucker. *Journal of Management History, 15*(4), 420–451. doi:10.1108/17511340910987338

Pfefferman, T. (2017). Reassembling the Archives: Business History Knowledge Production from an Actor-Network Perspective. *Management & Organizational History, 11*(4), 380–398.

Phillips, M. (2007). Midwives Versus Medics: A 17th-Century Professional Turf War. *Management & Organizational History, 2*(1), 27–44.

Phillips, M. (2010). A Tale of a Dog: Medieval Women Organizing Through Myth and Ritual. *Management & Organizational History, 5*(3–4), 296–313.

Phillips, M., & Rippin, A. (2010). Special Issue: Women in Management and Organizational History. *Management & Organizational History, 5*(3–4), 283–446.

Phipps, S. T. A. (2011). Mary, Mary, Quite Contrary. *Journal of Management History, 17*(3), 270–281.

Poor, S., Novicevic, M. M., Humphreys, J. H., & Popooola, I. T. (2016). Making History Happen: A Genealogical Analysis of Colt's Rhetorical History. *Management & Organizational History, 11*(2), 147–165.

Prasad, P & Prasad, A. (2002). The Coming of Age of Interpretive Organization Research), *Organizational Research Methods*, 2002, Vol. 5: 4–11.

Prieto, L. C. (2012). Women Issues to Wonder Woman. *Journal of Management History, 18*(2), 166–177. doi:10.1108/17511341211206834

Prieto, L. C., & Phipps, S. T. A. (2016). Re-discovering Charles Clinton Spaulding's "The Administration of Big Business". *Journal of Management History, 22*(1), 73–90.

Prieto, L. C., Phipps, S. T. A., Thompson, L. R., & Smith, X. A. (2016). Schneiderman, Perkins, and the Early Labor Movement. *Journal of Management History, 22*(1), 50–72.

Prasad, A. (1997). The Colonizing Consciousness and Representations of the Other: A Postcolonial Critique of the Discourse of Oil. In P. Prasad, A. J. Mills, M. Elmes, & A. Prasad (Eds.), *Managing the Organizational Melting Pot: Dilemmas of Workplace Diversity* (pp. 285–311). Thousand Oaks, CA: Sage.

Prasad, A. (Ed.). (2003). *Postcolonial Theory and Organizational Analysis: A Critical Engagement.* London: Palgrave.

Prasad, P. (2018). *Crafting Qualitative Research. Beyond Positivist Traditions.* London: Routledge.

Quinn, J. (2015). Editorial: Re-introducing Evolutionary Theory to Business History: Making Sense of Today's Structures. *Business History, 57*(5), 655–663.

Reed, M. (1990). From Paradigms to Images: The Paradigm Warrior Turns Post-modernist Guru. *Personnel Review, 19*(3), 35–40.

Rehn, A., & Rippin, A. (2010). "Rose's Turn" Female Careers in the Life (1908–1984) and Portrayals (1940–1959) of Ethel Merman. *Management & Organizational History, 5*(3–4), 349–359.

Ricoeur, P. (1984). *Time and Narrative.* Chicago, IL: Chicago University Press.

Rippin, A. (2013). Thirteen Notebooks for Walter Benjamin. *Management & Organizational History, 8*(1), 43–61.

Roethlisberger, F. J., & Dickson, W. J. (1939). *Management and the Worker.* Cambridge, MA: Harvard University Press.

Rose, M. (1978). *Industrial Behaviour.* Harmondsworth: Penguin.

Rose, S. O. (2010). *What is Gender History?* Cambridge: Polity Press.

Rostis, A. (2015). *Organizing Disaster: The Construction of Humanitarianism.* Bingley: Emerald Books.

Rowbotham, S. (1999). *A Century of Women. A History of Women in Britain and the United States.* London: Penguin.

Rowlinson, M. (1988). The Early Application of Scientific Management by Cadbury. *Business History, 30*(4), 377–395.

Rowlinson, M. (1995). Strategy, Structure and Culture – Cadbury, Divisionalization and Merger in the 1960s. *Journal of Management Studies, 32*(2), 121–140.

Rowlinson, M. (2004). Historical Perspectives in Organization Studies: Factual, Narrative, and Archaeo-Genealogical. In D. E. Hodgson & C. Carter (Eds.), *Management Knowledge and The New Employee* (pp. 8–20). Burlington, VT: Ashgate Publishing Company.

Rowlinson, M. (2015). Revisiting the Historic Turn: A Personal Reflection. In P. G. McLaren, J. Mills, & T. G. Weatherbee (Eds.), *The Routledge Companion to Management and Organizational History* (pp. 70–79). London: Routledge.

Rowlinson, M., & Hassard, J. (2013). Historical Neo-institutionalism or Neo-institutionalist History? *Management & Organizational History, 8*(2), 111–126.

Rowlinson, M., Hassard, J., & Decker, S. (2014). Strategies for Organizational History: A Dialogue between Historical Theory and Organizational History. *Academy of Management Review, 39*(3), 250–274.

Russell, J. (2015). Organization Men and Women: Making Managers at Bell Canada from the 1940s to the 1960s. *Management & Organizational History, 10*(3–4), 213–229.

Said, E. W. (1978). *Orientalism*. New York: Vintage Books.

Said, E. W. (1979). *Orientalism*. New York: Vintage.

Said, E. W. (1993). *Culture and Imperialism*. New York: Vintage.

Samuel, R. (2006). *The lost world of British communism*, Verso, NY.

Sanderson, K., Parsons, D. B., Helms Mills, J., & Mills, A. J. (2010). Riding the Second Wave: Organizing Feminism and Organizational Discourse – Stewardesses for Women's Rights. *Management & Organizational History, 5*(3–4), 360–377.

Sarsby, J. (1988). *Missuses & Mouldrunners: An Oral History of Women Pottery Workers at Work and at Home*. Milton Keynes: Open University Press.

Sartre, J. P. (1948). *Existentialism and humanism*. London: Methuen.

Sartre, J. P. (1957). *Being and Nothingness: An Essay on Phenomenological Ontology*. New York: Philosophical Library.

Schreyogg, G., Sydow, J., & Holtmann, P. (2011). How History Matters in Organizations: The Case of Path Dependence. *Management & Organizational History, 6*(1), 81–100.

Schwarzkopf, S. (2012). What is an Archive – and Where is It?: Why Business Historians Need a Constructive Theory of the Archive. *Business Archives, 105*(11), 1–9.

Scott, J. W. (1986). Gender: A useful category of historical analysis. *The American Historical Review, 91*(5), 1053–1075.

Scott, J. W. (1987). Rewriting History. In M. R. Higonnet, J. Jenson, S. Michel, & M. C. Weitz (Eds.), *Between the Lines. Gender and the two world wars* (pp. 19–30). London: Yale University Press.

Scott, J. W. (1990). *A Matter of Record*. Cambridge, MA: Polity.

Scott, J. W. (2007). History-Writing as critique. In K. Jenkins, S. Morgan, & A. Munslow (Eds.), *Manifestos for History* (pp. 19–38). London: Routledge.

Shaffner, E., Mills, A. J., & Helms Mills, J. (2017). Reading Qantas History: Discourses on Intersectionality and the Early Years of Qantas. In A. J. Mills (Ed.), *Insights and Reflections on the Study of Gender and Intersectionality in the Cultures of Airlines Overtime* (pp. 445–469). Bingley: Emerald.

Shenhav, Y., & Weitz, E. (2000). The Roots of Uncertainty in Organization Theory: A Historical Constructivist Analysis. *Organization, 7*(3), 373–401.

Sidani, Y. M. (2008). Ibn Khaldun of North Africa: An AD 1377 Theory of Leadership. *Journal of Management History, 14*(1), 73–86.

Sluyterman, K., & Bouwens, B. (2015). From Colonial Empires to Developing Countries and on to Emerging Economies: The International Expansion of the Dutch Brewery Heineken, 1930–2010. *Management & Organizational History, 10*(2), 103–118.

Smith, A., & Russell, J. (2016). Toward Polyphonic Constitutive Historicism: A New Research Agenda for Management Historians. *Management & Organizational History, 11*(2), 236–251. doi:10.1080/17449359.2015.1115742

Smith, A., & Simeone, D. (2017). Learning to Use the Past: The Development of a Rhetorical History Strategy by the London Headquarters of the Hudson Bay Company. *Management & Organizational History, 12*(4), 334–356.

Spivak, G. C. (1987). *In Other Worlds: Essays in Cultural Politics*. New York: Methuen.

Srinivas, L. (2010). Ladies queues, 'roadside Romeos,' and balcony seating: Ethnographic observations on women's cinema-going experiences. *South Asian Popular Culture* 8.3 (2010): 291–307.

Stan, L. (2010). Archival Records as Evidence. In A. J. Mills, G. Durepos, & E. Weibe (Eds.), *Sage Encyclopedia of Case Study Research* (pp. 29–31). Thousand Oaks, CA: Sage.

Suddaby, R., Foster, W., & Mills, A. J. (2014). Historical Institutionalism. In M. Bucheli & D. Wadhwani (Eds.), *Organizations in Time* (pp. 100–123). Oxford: Oxford University Press.

Tancred-Sheriff, P., & Campbell, E. J. (1992). Room for Women: A Case Study in the Sociology of Organizations. In A. J. Mills & P. Tancred (Eds.), *Gendering Organizational Analysis* (pp. 31–45). Newbury Park, CA: Sage.

Taylor, N. (2008). *American-made. The Enduring Legacy of the WPA*. New York: Bantam Dell.

Taylor, S., Bell, E., & Cooke, B. (2009). Business History and the Historiographical Operation. *Management & Organizational History, 4*(2), 151–166.

Thomas, R., Mills, A. J., & Helms Mills, J. (2004). *Identity Politics at Work: Resisting Gender, Gendering Resistance*. London: Routledge.

Thompson, E. P. (1983). An Interview with Mike Merrill. In H. Abelove, B. Blackmar, P. Dimock, & J. Schneer (Eds.), *Visions of History* (pp. 5–25). New York: Pantheon Books.

Toms, S., & Wilson, J. (2010). In Defence of Business History: A Reply to Taylor, Bell and Cooke. *Management & Organizational History, 5*(1), 109–120.

Urwick, L. (1938). The Development of Scientific Management in Great Britain. A Report Distributed to Members of the Seventh International Management Congress, 1938, London. *British Management Review, III*(4), pp. 18–96. Reprinted as a separate booklet.

Urwick, L., & Brech, E. F. L. (1944). *The Human Factor in Management 1795–1943*. London: Institute of Labour Management.

Urwick, L., & Brech, E. F. L. (1957a). *The Making of Scientific Management. Management in British Industry* (Vol. II). London: Sir Isaac Pitman & Sons, Ltd.

Urwick, L., & Brech, E. F. L. (1957b). *The Making of Scientific Management. The Hawthorne Investigations* (Vol. III). London: Sir Isaac Pitman & Sons Ltd.

Urwick, L., & Brech, E. F. L. (1957c). *The Making of Scientific Management. Thirteen Pioneers* (Vol. I). London: Sir Isaac Pitman & Sons Ltd.

Usdiken, B., & Kieser, A. (2004). Introduction: History in Organization Studies. *Business History, 46*(3), 321–330.

van den Broek, Diane. (2011). Strapping, as Well as Numerate: Occupational Identity, Masculinity and the Aesthetics of Nineteenth-Century Banking. *Business History, 53*(3), 289–301.

Wall, Christine. (2010). Something to Show for It: The Place of Momentoes in Women's Oral Histories. *Management & Organizational History, 5*(3–4), 378–394.

Wanderley, S., & Barros, A. (2018). Decoloniality, Geopolitics of Knowledge and Historic Turn: Towards a Latin American Agenda. *Management & Organizational History, 14*(1), 79–97.

Wanderley, S., & Faria, A. (2012). The Chadler-Furtado Case: A De-colonial Re-framing of a North/South (Did)Encounter. *Management & Organizational History, 7*(3), 219–236.

Webb, E. J., Campbell, D. T., Schwartz, R. D., & Sechrest, L. (1984). The Use of Archival Sources in Social Research. In M. Bulmer (Ed.), *Sociological Research Methods.* (pp. 113–130). London: Macmillan.

Whipp, R., & Clark, P. (1986). *Innovation and the Auto Industry: Product, Process and Work Organization.* London: Francis Pinter.

White, A. (2015). On the Birth of a Nation's Centenary. *National Review.* Accessed at: www.nationalreview.com/2015/02/birth-nations-centenary-armond-white/

White, H. (1973). *Metahistory: The Historical Imagination in Nineteenth-Century Europe.* Balitimore, MD: The Johns Hopkins University Press.

White, H. (1984). The Question of Narrative in Contemporary Historical Theory. *History and Theory, 23*(1), 1–33.

White, H. (1987). *The Content of the Form: Narrative Discourse and Historical Representation.* London: John Hopkins University Press.

Whitehead, T. N. (1938). *The Industrial Worker.* Oxford: Oxford Press.

Whittle, A., & Wilson, J. (2015). Ethnomethodology and the Production of History: Studying 'History-In-Action'. *Business History, 57*(1), 41–63.

Willett, J. (2011). Book Review: Knights of the Razor: Black Barbers in Slavery and Freedom, by Douglas Walter Bristol, Jr, Baltimore, MD, The Johns Hopkins University Press, 2009. *Business History, 53*(3), 467–469.

Williams, K. S., & Mills, A. J. (2017). Frances Perkins: Gender, Context and History in the Neglect of a Management Theorist. *Journal of Management History, 23*(1), 32–50. doi:10.1108/jmh-09–2016–0055

Williams, K. S., & Mills, A. J. (2018). Hallie Flanagan and the Federal Theater Project: A Critical Undoing of Management History. *Journal of Management History, 24*(3), 282–299.

Willmott, H. (1993). Breaking the Paradigm Mentality. *Organization Studies, 14*(5), 681–719.

Wolff, J. (1977). Women in Organizations. In S. Clegg & D. Dunkerley (Eds.), *Critical Issues in Organizations* (pp. 7–20). London: Routeledge & Kegan Paul.

Weatherbee, T. G. (2012). Caution! This Historiography Makes Wide Turns: Historic Turns and Breaks in Management and Organization Studies. *Management & Organizational History, 7*(3), 203–218.

Wren, D. A. (1972). *The Evolution of Management Thought* (First ed.). New York: The Ronald Press Co.

Wren, D. A. (1979). *The Evolution of Management Thought* (Second ed.). New York: The Ronald Press Co.

Wren, D. A., & Bedeian, A. G. (2009). *The Evolution of Management Thought* (Sixth ed.). Hoboken, NJ: John Wiley & Sons, Inc.

Wren, D. A., & Bedeian, A. G. (2018). *The Evolution of Management Thought* (Seventh ed.). Hoboken, NJ: John Wiley & Sons, Inc.

Yin, R. K. (2009). *Case Study Research. Design and Methods* (Fourth ed.). Thousand Oaks, CA: Sage.

Zald, M. N. (1989). History, Theory and the Sociology of Organizations. In J. E. Jackson (Ed.), *American Society: Essays in Market, Political and Social Organizations* (pp. 81–108). Ann Arbor: University of Michigan Press.

Zald, M. N. (1993). Organization Studies as a Scientific and Humanistic Enterprise: Toward a Reconceptualization of the Foundations of the Field. *Organization Science, 4*(4), 513–528.

Zald, M. N. (2002). Spinning Disciplines: Critical Management Studies in the Context of the Transformation of Management Education. *Organization, 9*, 365–385.

Zinn, H. (1990). *The Politics of History* (Second ed.). Urbana and Chicago: University of Illinois Press.

Zinn, H. (1997). The Politics of History in the Era of the Cold War. In N. Chomsky (Ed.), *The Cold War & The University* (pp. 35–72). New York: The New Press.

Zundel, M., Holt, R., & Popp, A. (2016). Using History in the Creation of Organizational Identity. *Management & Organizational History*, 1–25. doi:10.1080/17449359.2015.1124042

Index

Note: page numbers followed by "n" denote endnotes.